Stephen King

The People to Know Series

Madeleine Albright
*First Woman
Secretary of State*
0-7660-1143-7

Neil Armstrong
*The First Man
on the Moon*
0-89490-828-6

Isaac Asimov
*Master of
Science Fiction*
0-7660-1031-7

Robert Ballard
*Oceanographer Who
Discovered the* Titanic
0-7660-1147-X

Willa Cather
Writer of the Prairie
0-89490-980-0

Bill Clinton
*United States
President*
0-89490-437-X

Hillary Rodham Clinton
Activist First Lady
0-89490-583-X

Bill Cosby
Actor and Comedian
0-89490-548-1

Walt Disney
*Creator of
Mickey Mouse*
0-89490-694-1

Bob Dole
Legendary Senator
0-89490-825-1

Marian Wright Edelman
*Fighting for
Children's Rights*
0-89490-623-2

Bill Gates
*Billionaire
Computer Genius*
0-89490-824-3

Jane Goodall
Protector of Chimpanzees
0-89490-827-8

Al Gore
*Leader for the
New Millennium*
0-7660-1232-8

Tipper Gore
*Activist, Author,
Photographer*
0-7660-1142-9

Ernest Hemingway
Writer and Adventurer
0-89490-979-7

Ron Howard
*Child Star &
Hollywood Director*
0-89490-981-9

John F. Kennedy
*President of the
New Frontier*
0-89490-693-3

Stephen King
*King of Thrillers
and Horror*
0-7660-1233-6

John Lennon
The Beatles and Beyond
0-89490-702-6

Maya Lin
Architect and Artist
0-89490-499-X

Jack London
*A Writer's
Adventurous Life*
0-7660-1144-5

Barbara McClintock
*Nobel Prize
Geneticist*
0-89490-983-5

Rosie O'Donnell
*Talk Show Host
and Comedian*
0-7660-1148-8

Christopher Reeve
*Hollywood's Man
of Courage*
0-7660-1149-6

Ann Richards
*Politician, Feminist,
Survivor*
0-89490-497-3

Sally Ride
*First American Woman
in Space*
0-89490-829-4

Will Rogers
Cowboy Philosopher
0-89490-695-X

Franklin D. Roosevelt
*The Four-Term
President*
0-89490-696-8

Steven Spielberg
Hollywood Filmmaker
0-89490-697-6

John Steinbeck
America's Author
0-7660-1150-X

Martha Stewart
*Successful
Businesswoman*
0-89490-984-3

Amy Tan
Author of
The Joy Luck Club
0-89490-699-2

Alice Walker
Author of
The Color Purple
0-89490-620-8

Simon Wiesenthal
*Tracking Down
Nazi Criminals*
0-89490-830-8

Frank Lloyd Wright
Visionary Architect
0-7660-1032-5

People to Know

Stephen King

King of Thrillers and Horror

Suzan Wilson

Enslow Publishers, Inc.

40 Industrial Road	PO Box 38
Box 398	Aldershot
Berkeley Heights, NJ 07922	Hants GU12 6BP
USA	UK

http://www.enslow.com

To Nina, for making it all possible

Library of Congress Cataloging-in-Publication Data

Wilson, Suzan.
    Stephen King—king of thrillers and horror / Suzan Wilson.
        p.   cm. — (People to know)
    Includes bibliographical references and index.
    "Books by Stephen King": p. 112
    Summary: Traces the life of a popular novelist, from his childhood as an avid
reader to his current success as a creator of horror fiction.
    ISBN 0-7660-1233-6
    1. King, Stephen, 1947–   . Juvenile literature. 2. Novelists, American—20th
century Biography Juvenile literature. 3. Horror tales—Authorship Juvenile
literature. [1. King, Stephen, 1947–   . 2. Authors, American.] I. Title. II. Series.
PS3561.I483Z92   2000
813'.54—dc21
[B]   99-33545
                                                                                              CIP

Printed in the United States of America

10 9 8 7 6 5 4 3 .

To Our Readers:
All Internet addresses in this book were active and appropriate when we went to press.
Any comments or suggestions can be sent by e-mail to Comments@enslow.com or to
the address on the back cover.

Illustration Credits: © 1998 by George Beahm, p. 107; Bangor Daily News
Photo, pp. 40, 57, 66, 77, 80, 83, 88, 93, 96, 98, 105; Courtesy of The
Stanley Hotel, p. 10; Enslow Publishers, Inc., p. 70; Illustration by Howard
Pyle, p. 19; NASA, p. 23; Suzan Wilson, pp. 26, 30, 32, 36, 74; Willa Belcher,
pp. 46, 49.

Cover Illustration: © 1999 Virginia Sherwood/ABC, Inc.

Contents

Acknowledgment

The author wishes to thank Stephen King, Marsha DeFilippo, and Juliann Eugley, who so graciously answered questions.

Horror at the Stanley Hotel

On the day before Halloween in 1974, Stephen King's mind felt as barren as the trees outside his Boulder, Colorado, home. The story he was writing was not developing the way he had hoped, so he and his wife, Tabitha, decided to take a short vacation. The Stanley Hotel in Estes Park, Colorado, would be the perfect place. It sounded quaint and relaxing. Plus, it was close to their two children in case of an emergency. The trip turned out to be an experience right out of one of his books. Stephen King, horror writer on vacation, spent a haunting twenty-four hours in a remote hotel. As a result, he wrote a best-seller.

Signs along the narrow, mountain highway into Estes Park warned that roads might be closed by snow any time after October 15.[1] Green-needled fir and pine trees shuddered in the wind, and bare aspen trees stretched their skeleton arms skyward, waiting to catch the first snow of the season. The sixty-five-year-old Stanley Hotel stood at the crest of a hill, its long narrow drive winding up from the highway. The Colorado Rockies rose grandly behind the hotel, but on this day clouds hid the mountains, leaving the Stanley Hotel in eerie solitude.

The Kings had their choice of parking spaces. All the other guests were leaving. A few took last-minute pictures of the old Stanley Steamer car parked out front, but no one strolled leisurely around the grounds. The lobby was quiet. No one sat reading, writing letters, or sharing stories. Stephen and Tabitha King were the only guests that night. The tourist season was over. The hotel was isolated, and anyone there after the first snow could be stranded until spring cleared the roads again.[2]

The staff was busy closing up rooms and packing away supplies for the winter. Even the credit card slips had been sent off. King searched through his pockets for enough cash to pay for their stay.[3] As the couple walked down the long corridor toward Room 217, King's imagination went wild. "We were the only guests, and we could hear the wind screaming outside."[4] Coils of fire hoses hung rigidly on the wall of the old building, but in King's mind the hoses came alive—not full of water to put out fires, but like snakes thumping against the carpet and chasing after him. Terrifying readers was his business. Now he felt the terror and he loved it.[5]

Later, in the dining room, an orchestra of tuxedoed musicians played for the two guests, but the dance floor remained empty.[6] Tables stacked with chairs, legs awry, were covered with plastic sheets.

After dinner, Tabitha returned to their room, and King sat at the bar. His imagination had been turned on and he could not relax. Later, alone in the maze of corridors, King lost his way. The wind howled up and down the hallways, doors seemed to open, and threatening patterns seemed to appear on the carpet.

When he finally found Room 217, King thought a bath would help his mind settle down. As he sat in the deep, steaming water of the old-fashioned claw-footed bathtub, his body relaxed and he fell asleep. Perhaps the water flowing onto his face as he slipped beneath the surface awoke him. Suddenly, he was up and out of the tub, thinking how close he had come to drowning. "What if somebody died here?" he asked himself.[7] Then he knew that all the strange experiences of the day could be tied together for a new book.

Since 1962, King had been developing a story he eventually called *The Shining*. In it, dreams, bad dreams, came alive. "I wanted to take a little kid with his family and put them someplace, cut off, where spooky things would happen."[8] He first thought of a haunted amusement park, but the family could not be isolated the way he wanted. As he looked at the bathtub in Room 217, thought of the Road Closed signs, the deserted hotel with its endless maze of corridors and fire hoses that seemed to thump in the hall, he knew the setting and the horrors of his next novel.[9]

King set *The Shining* in a hotel similar to the Stanley. The winter caretaker of the fictitious Overlook Hotel is Jack Torrance, the alcoholic father of a family with lots of problems. Fear causes Jack to go crazy while snowed in at the remote mountaintop resort. Many dreams, bad dreams, become real. Tuxedoed ghouls play music while ghosts and zombies dance. Fire hoses chase victims down the hall. And a ghost haunts the bathtub in Room 217.

The Shining, King's fourth novel, was published in

As the resort closed for the winter season, the eerie solitude of the Stanley Hotel in Estes Park, Colorado, sparked the imagination of Stephen King. Readers would visit a similar hotel in his chilling novel The Shining.

1977. It became an instant best-seller. Three years later it was made into a movie, but King did not like the changes director Stanley Kubrick made in the script. In 1996, King went back to the Stanley Hotel to make his own version of *The Shining* as a television miniseries.

The cast and crew of the new movie filled all the rooms in the old hotel. They talked of ghosts, real ghosts that turned doorknobs and made mysterious thumping noises. No one wanted to stay in Room 217, a place many thought held dark secrets. Only one room was left when Courtland Mead, the ten-year-old actor playing a psychic boy, signed in. It was Room 217. A staff member taped the number 222 over 217, and Courtland never knew.[10]

Stephen King was happy with the budget and the freedom ABC gave him to make the six-hour television miniseries, rated TV-14. The plot followed the book more closely than the original movie, but some frightening scenes were cut from the final version. In one of these scenes, the face of the ghoulish bandleader starts melting. Green ooze squirts from the side of his head, his right cheek drops to the floor, and an ear falls off. The man beneath the melting mask was Stephen King, trying to be part of the scariest movie ever made for TV.[11] Although this scene and others just as horrifying were cut, *The Shining* still terrified millions of viewers across North America. The miniseries cost $23 million to make and was first shown on TV in the spring of 1997. Many people videotaped the show so they could watch it more comfortably—in daylight.

Stephen King has published horror stories since 1967. His books, beginning with *Carrie* in 1974, have sold millions of copies throughout the world, and people have lined up to see dozens of his movies. Does he ever plan to quit writing? Only if he runs out of stories—and he still finds stories wherever he goes.

Or do the stories find him?

Tastes of Terror

Stephen Edwin King was born on September 21, 1947, in Portland, Maine. His parents, Nellie "Ruth" Pillsbury King and Donald Edwin King, took him home to Scarborough, a small town about ten miles south of Portland.

Maine was still recovering from World War II. New cars had not been made during the war, and repairs to machinery and property had been postponed. The war years, 1941 to 1945, had been difficult for all Americans, but by 1947, things were looking up. Rubber, steel, and sugar were once again easy to get. Businesses prospered. Families like the Kings seemed to have a bright future.

Ruth and Donald King had thought they were unable to have children of their own. Two years earlier, while living in New York, they had adopted a newborn baby boy.[1] David Victor King was Stephen's big brother.

Ruth King had married her husband when she was twenty-six, and she was in her midthirties when Stephen was born. She was related to the Pillsbury family, one of the big names in bakery products. She had studied piano at a music school in New York and had played the organ for a radio show in New York City.[2] Her playing could be heard live on radio throughout the United States and Canada. After David's adoption, the Kings had moved back to Maine to be near Ruth King's family.

Donald King had joined the Merchant Marine during World War II and was a captain when Stephen was born. He served on ships that transported people and supplies for the military. Although his ship was not a combat ship during the war, it was still in danger of being attacked and sunk. Soon after Stephen's birth, Donald King resigned from the Merchant Marine. Back in Maine, he worked at various jobs, including selling vacuum cleaners door-to-door, but he never found anything that suited him like the Merchant Marine. He had difficulty settling into family life. One night when Stephen was two years old, Donald King said he was going out to buy a pack of cigarettes and he never came back.[3]

Now, without a husband to support the family, Ruth had to arrange for the care of her two boys until she found a job that would support them. Her sister Ethelyn Flaws agreed to care for Stephen. Ethelyn lived with her husband, Oren, in Durham, Maine, in an old farmhouse with lots of nooks and crannies.

Four-year-old David stayed with Molly, another of Ruth's sisters, in Malden, Massachusetts.[4]

Ruth King searched unsuccessfully for a good job. Organ players were not in demand around Portland, Maine, and all the jobs that paid a decent wage were offered to men who had been soldiers and sailors during the war. Women were now expected to stay home and care for their families, not take jobs outside the home. Few women worked, and even fewer were single mothers. Consequently, Ruth accepted a series of unskilled jobs that never paid enough to provide her and the boys with a comfortable living.

After a few months, Ruth King collected her boys, and for four years they all lived with relatives while looking for a place to call home. In Chicago, Illinois, they lived with Donald King's mother. The relatives they lived with in West De Pere, Wisconsin, had a dog. When the boys played in the yard there, they had to be careful to stay away from messy dog piles. In Fort Wayne, Indiana, they lived with Donald King's sister, Betty, who was a schoolteacher. After Ruth King got a good job in Fort Wayne at the General Electric factory, winding coils for small motors, she and her sons were able to move into their own apartment. At other times, Ruth King worked as a doughnut maker, a presser in a laundry, a store clerk, and a housekeeper. One job had a benefit Stephen and David enjoyed. When she worked the night shift at a bakery, she brought home broken cookies for dessert.[5] Otherwise, she could not afford desserts.

When Stephen was four years old, he experienced two traumatic events. First, he collided with a hockey

Ruth King with her two sons, David, age 7, and Stephen, 5.

player, hit his head on the ice, and was knocked out.[6] He revived on his own after five minutes, but everyone, including his mother, was frightened by the incident.

Stephen never remembered the second event. His mother told him that one day he had come home deadly pale. He had wet his pants. He solemnly went to his room and stayed alone all day. He would not talk to her. Ruth King later learned that the friend Stephen was playing with had been run over by a freight train.[7] It was a gruesome accident, and Ruth King was concerned that Stephen may have seen his friend's body being shattered by the train and then scattered along the tracks.

Just before Stephen turned six, the family moved to Stratford, Connecticut, and he started kindergarten at Center School. David had entered kindergarten before his fifth birthday and had skipped second grade with the encouragement of his Aunt Betty back in Fort Wayne, so he was in fourth grade now.[8] The boys, only two years apart in age, were four years apart in school. The family lived briefly with Ruth King's sister Gert and then found a place of their own on West Broad Street. Ruth King worked in a laundry while the boys were in school.

No matter where they lived, Ruth King spent many hours entertaining her sons with stories. Few of their relatives had television, so evenings were spent telling tales, reading books, and listening to the radio. One night when Stephen was six, he sneaked out of bed so he could listen to a radio show called *Dimension X.*

That night's story was "Mars Is Heaven" by writer Ray Bradbury. This tale caused shivers in the bravest adult. Stephen's mother refused to let him listen, but once she thought he was in bed, she turned on the radio. Stephen opened the door a bit and pressed his ear against the crack. The story terrified him, but he did not let her know. He spent the night curled up on the hall floor, where the light of the bathroom protected him from his imagination.[9]

Ruth King introduced the boys to great books by reading stories from "Classics Illustrated," comic books that retold famous stories such as *Treasure Island*.[10] She loved horror stories, and when Stephen was seven, he easily talked his mother into reading him Robert Louis Stevenson's *The Strange Case of Dr. Jekyll and Mr. Hyde*. They read the book on the porch that summer. It was instantly his favorite and one of the first books he read himself. He read it over and over and decided he wanted to write horror stories too. "I have to do that," he said to himself, "but I have to do it worse."[11]

The Kings had little money for entertainment, but one evening Milt, a man Ruth was dating, took the family to the drive-in movies. David fell asleep on the floor of Milt's Buick, but Stephen sat captivated by *The Creature from the Black Lagoon*. Even at that age, he knew the monster on the screen was a man in a monster suit with a zipper up the back, but he worried that maybe the creature would visit him later in the night. What if it hid in a closet or slumped in the shadows, waiting to gobble him up for a midnight snack?[12]

After reading The Strange Case of Dr. Jekyll and Mr. Hyde, *illustrated above, Stephen decided he would write horror stories too—but "worse" ones.*

Stephen put his vivid imagination to work in first grade when he wrote a science fiction story about a dinosaur that terrorized a town. Fortunately, a scientist learns that dinosaurs are allergic to leather. The townspeople torment the dinosaur with leather items until it goes away. All the elements of good story plotting were there. First, something strange happens. Then, scientists discover a unique explanation, which is not necessarily based on facts. Finally, the solution works and the horror goes away.[13]

Stephen's Aunt Gert rewarded him for each story he wrote. When he was nine, she gave him a quarter for writing a fairy tale called "Jhonathan and the Witches." A grumpy king orders Jhonathan to kill three witches or he will lose his head. Jhonathan succeeds in a clever manner and is given five thousand crowns so he and his father can live happily ever after. Who could imagine then that the first page of this fairy tale would one day be reprinted in a collection of early writings by famous authors, called *First Words* (Algonquin Books, 1993).

Stephen read constantly and discovered that children's fantasy stories could be as unpredictable and terrifying as adult horror stories. *The 500 Hats of Bartholomew Cubbins* by Dr. Seuss demonstrated that strange things can happen to the most ordinary people for no apparent reason.[14] Stephen found fairy tales very frightening. What could be more horrifying than not having enough to eat; being abandoned by one's parents, imprisoned by a wicked old lady, and threatened with cannibalism; and having one's mother die? Yet the story of *Hansel and Gretel* still thrills parents and children. Few recognize it as a horror tale because it was written for children.

Other stories terrified Stephen even more because he was taught that they were true.[15] He read tales of gigantic floods, famine, diseases, human sacrifice, jealousy, and murder. These were stories from the Bible, the book used by his Methodist church to teach people, including children, about right and wrong, good and evil, and reward and punishment.

Stephen's other childhood fears came from his dreams and imagination. He worried that when he stood to salute the flag, his pants would fall down.[16] After watching a horror movie, he wondered, "What if that thing comes and gets me?"[17] He was afraid of ghosts, the bogeyman, and the dark. These are fears that haunt many children.

School did not go smoothly for Stephen. He earned good grades, but he was always the biggest and oldest in his class. He was pudgy and wore thick glasses, just as his father had. When the kids played games, he was always picked last. When he joined a game, he heard the other team taunt, "Ha, ha, you got King."[18]

Reading was an escape from an unstable life, and it was Stephen's favorite entertainment. But the Kings had no money to buy books. Stephen King later said that the only hardback books he read were library books.[19] They visited the Stratford public library frequently.

Ruth King also escaped into books. One day she bought an armful of used paperbacks for five cents each. The covers were torn off, but the stories were still good. When Stephen asked what she had, his mother said, "I've got a pile of cheap, sweet vacations."[20] Stephen liked pleasing his mother by giving her a paperback book for special occasions like her birthday or Mother's Day.

Stephen loved rock and roll music. He listened to it on the radio, and when he could, he watched *American Bandstand* on television. On the show, records introduced the newest songs, teenagers danced, entertainers made live appearances, and new dances and fashions were broadcast around the United States. One Christmas when Stephen was nine or ten, his mother gave him an Elvis Presley record. On one side was "Hound Dog" and on the other was "Don't Be Cruel." He played the Elvis songs over and over, until he had worn out the grooves in the record.[21]

The King brothers went to the movies as often as possible. Stephen told his mother he was seeing something like *Bambi* or *Davy Crockett*, but he usually saw a horror movie instead.[22] One Saturday in October 1957, eleven-year-old Stephen was watching *Earth vs. the Flying Saucers*. The theater lights suddenly came on. The audience started booing, but the manager of the theater calmed everyone down to make an announcement. The Soviet Union had launched a satellite called *Sputnik 1* into space.

Americans were worried about a possible war with the Soviet Union. Some people had built underground bomb shelters in their backyards, and schools had air-raid drills so students would know what to do if their town was attacked. Launching *Sputnik 1* meant

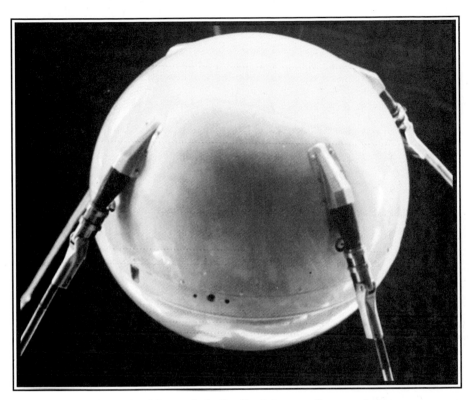

With the launch of Sputnik 1, *the Soviets won the race into space. If a war broke out, would they win that, too? worried young Stephen King.*

that the Soviets had better technology than the United States and that if a war started, the Soviet Union was likely to win. The United States immediately put more money into scientific research, made the space program a priority, and introduced new science and math courses in schools.

By the beginning of the next school year, the United States had launched its first satellite and the Kings had moved to Durham, Maine, the town Stephen King would call his boyhood home.

3

Moving Around

In 1958, Ruth King's relatives made a decision. Her mother and father, Guy and Nellie Fogg Pillsbury, could no longer manage living on their own. They needed someone to care for them in their old age. The relatives offered Ruth King a place to live and living expenses if she would care for her parents. She packed up the boys and their possessions and moved to Durham, Maine. Aunt Ethelyn and Uncle Oren Flaws lived just down the road in the same house Stephen had stayed in when he was two. Cousins and other relatives also lived nearby.

The house sat near a busy intersection. Highways led travelers north to Lewiston, east to Lisbon Falls, and south to Freeport and Portland. Durham had no town center. Narrow country roads linked fields, farmhouses, and forests. Churches were scattered throughout the community. Durham had one school and nine cemeteries. Residents grew much of their own food, found entertainment through church or clubs, and, when they had to, shopped in a neighboring town—at least six miles away.

Stephen's grandparents—he called them Daddy Guy and Mama—lived together in the parlor of their old house. It was the biggest room in the house and had been converted to a bed-sitting room. Daddy Guy had once worked as a handyman for Winslow Homer, a famous artist who settled on the Maine coast. Now eighty-two, Daddy Guy was fairly healthy and strong and got around on his own. He had a heavy beard and no teeth. No one except his daughter Ruth could understand what he said.[1] Mama was blind and spent all of her time in bed. She spoke clearly, but what she said made little sense. Mostly she talked of people and experiences from the past.[2]

Stephen, eleven, and David, thirteen, moved into an upstairs bedroom, which they shared for the next four years. Looking out their window, they could see the Methodist church next door. Just beyond it was Stephen's school, a one-room building for children from kindergarten to eighth grade. Behind their house was an outhouse. Although they had indoor plumbing, they needed the outhouse when the well went dry. "We called the outhouse The Blue Room, because of its hideous blue paint job," recalled King later.[3] He thought it was a good place to reflect upon life, but it was horribly uncomfortable and was particularly inconvenient during winter storms.[4]

Every summer, the well at the Pillsburys' old house went dry for a month or so. Stephen and David helped their uncle get water from the town pump. Oren Flaws had made a large tank, which they set on the tailgate of an old station wagon. The boys carried big steel milk cans full of water from the pump to the tank. It was hard work, but necessary because the Pillsburys could not afford to have a new well drilled.

Uncle Clayt lived nearby and visited often. He shared hundreds of stories with Stephen: Indian stories, ghost stories, family stories, and legends. Uncle

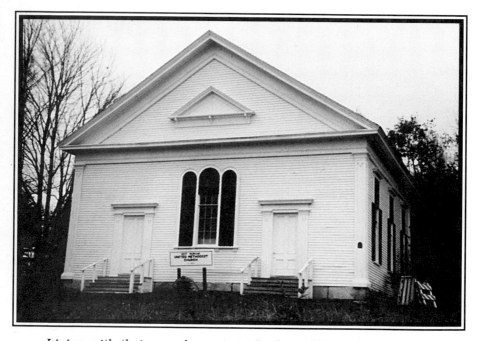

Living with their grandparents in Durham, Maine, Stephen and David shared an upstairs bedroom. Looking out the window, Stephen could see this Methodist church next door.

Clayt also dowsed for water. He took his apple-wood dowsing rod out to the Pillsburys' yard one summer day when Stephen was twelve. He patiently showed his nephew how to hold the wishbone-shaped rod and walk back and forth across the yard. Uncle Clayt believed the rod could sense water and would turn down on its own, pointing to a place where water ran close to the surface. He found a spot and then handed the dowsing rod to his nephew. Stephen walked back and forth across the yard until he felt the rod straining against his hands. The dowsing stick turned down at the same place it had for Uncle Clayt. Stephen could not believe what had happened. Four years later, a new well was drilled on that very spot. Water was found within one hundred feet of the surface, and the well never went dry again.[5]

The Pillsburys had no television, but Daddy Guy owned a radio. Stephen would bring in a chair and join his grandfather in his corner of the room.[6] Daddy Guy would light a huge cigar, turn on one of his favorite programs, and enjoy his grandson's company. They listened to programs such as *Gunsmoke*, a western, and suspense thrillers like *Inner Sanctum*. Several years later both became popular television shows. After a neighborhood family bought a television set, Stephen visited there frequently to watch Marshall Dillon and Chester defend the western town of Dodge on *Gunsmoke*. Now Stephen no longer needed to imagine the eerily creaking door that introduced *Inner Sanctum*. It was a relief to finally see it, cobwebs and all. Stephen King recalled, "Nothing could have looked as horrible as that door *sounded*."[7]

Houses were far apart in Durham, and residents stayed in touch through phone calls. The Pillsburys shared a telephone line with seven other homes. If someone was talking, anyone else on the party line, as it was called, could pick up the phone and hear what was being said. Stephen said he could hear the noisy breathing of the old lady up the street when he talked to a girlfriend.[8]

The first January the Kings lived in Durham, the brothers found another way for the neighbors to stay in touch. Together with their cousin Donald Flaws, they started a neighborhood newspaper called "Dave's Rag." The boys typed their paper on an old typewriter that did not have an "n" key. After writing stories, they had to go back and fill in every missing "n." In the beginning, each copy of the newspaper was individually typed, which took a lot of time.[9] After a few issues, Ruth gave David an old mimeograph copying machine, which he set up in the basement. The crank that turned the machine was broken, so the boys had to turn the cylinder by hand.[10] "Dave's Rag," a twice-monthly publication, had a peak circulation of twenty paid households. Stephen King, only twelve years old, was in the publishing business.

David V. King was the editor-in-chief and illustrator of "Dave's Rag." Stephen E. King acted as a reporter, and Donald P. Flaws covered the local sports. The paper consisted of social news such as birthdays or out-of-town guests, weather, jokes, letters, classified ads, editorials, church news, and illustrations. A local newspaper, the *Brunswick Record*, interviewed the boys for a feature article printed on April 23, 1959. The last issue of "Dave's Rag" came out in October 1959. It was their Summer Special and included reports on summer vacations, the World Series (the Dodgers beat the White Sox), and paid advertisements. One ad read:

> New book by STEVE KING! "Thirty-One of the Classics"! Read "Kidnapped," "Tom Sawyer," and many others!!! If you order in three weeks, only 30¢. Contact Steve King % Dave's Rag.[11]

In addition to advertising recreated classics, Stephen wrote a review of the new fall TV programs. All the neighborhood kids crowded into one living room to watch television. Stephen watched as often as he could and wrote reviews for *Trouble Shooters, Five Fingers, The Deputy, Man from Blackhawk,* and two science fiction shows, *Man Into Space* and *The Twilight Zone.* "There's T.V. for every fan," he reported.[12]

That was the last issue. David and Donald started their second year at Brunswick High School, riding to school in the back of Oren Flaw's pickup. Stephen read and wrote during his spare time.

Stephen was twelve and a sixth grader when ten-year-old Chris Chesley transferred to the West Durham School. The Chesley family lived midway between two one-room schools, and his parents decided to transfer Chris to West Durham at the beginning of fifth grade. Chris wanted to read some of Stephen's stories, but Stephen was reluctant to show a new kid, especially a fifth grader, his writing. Chris insisted and was immediately impressed by Stephen King's talent.[13]

The one-room schoolhouse that Stephen attended is now a private residence.

Stephen and Chris spent a lot of time together, much of it writing. At first one would write a paragraph or two and then the other would take over for a few paragraphs. Sometimes they would rewrite stories, using words and scenes that made readers feel as if they were watching a movie.[14]

By 1960, when they were thirteen and eleven, Stephen and Chris had accumulated a number of one-page horror stories, and they decided to self-publish a book titled *People, Places, and Things*. Calling themselves Triad Publishing Company, they typed up the stories, made copies on the old mimeograph in the basement, and sold them to interested people.[15] Their stories were "strongly influenced by *The Twilight Zone*," King later recalled.[16]

Stephen and Chris also enjoyed reading together. They liked long, seventy-five-cent dramatic novels as well as science fiction and horror tales.[17] Because Stephen and David's bedroom had no bookcase, the King boys organized their paperback books on the floor against the walls of the room, spines up, so they could read the titles.[18]

Ruth King had a way of getting things that would interest her boys. First, she had found the typewriter with the missing "n," then the broken mimeograph machine, and now she gave David an eight-millimeter movie camera. Stephen and Chris borrowed it to make a haunted house movie, using a vacant, run-down house in the neighborhood as the set. They climbed through a broken window to shoot inside. They agreed that it was not especially scary in the daylight, but neither volunteered to spend the night there alone.

They did spend nights in the graveyard, though. Stephen and Chris climbed out their bedroom windows at midnight to visit the cemetery just one hundred yards from Chris's house. They looked at the big and little monuments, read dates and final words, and mentally tallied the ages at death. They found as many children buried in the cemetery as old people. Sitting on the low stone wall surrounding the cemetery, the friends wondered why so many people died so young.[19]

In the summer, Stephen and his friends rowed a boat or a homemade raft out to the middle of the river

One of the nine cemeteries in Durham. Stephen and his best friend, Chris Chesley, would sneak into a nearby cemetery at night to read the gravestones.

to swim. Sometimes they persuaded visitors to wade into the inviting shallow water near shore. Once in the water, strangers found out that snapping turtles, greasy eels, and bloodsucking leeches lurked in the muddy bottom. Waders quickly made for shore to peel the leeches off their bodies.

Around this time, just before Stephen turned thirteen, he and Chris heard about a fisherman who had fallen out of his boat and drowned. The boys wanted to see his body. They sat on nearby rocks and watched the police and medical people take pictures, write notes, and stand around the man lying dead on the shore. They never got close to the body, but they stared at it from a distance, thinking it looked inhuman. Finally, the officials covered the body, and the boys went home.[20]

Even though David and Stephen knew many of their father's relatives, the brothers knew little about their father. They once found a reel of movie film that their father had taken on shipboard before either boy was born. The brothers pooled their money to rent a movie projector and watched it over and over. Most of the scenes were of the ship, but one showed Donald King smiling and waving.[21]

When Stephen was twelve or thirteen, the brothers were exploring Aunt Ethelyn's house and came across some old boxes hidden away in the garage attic. To their surprise, David and Stephen found a book on seamanship, a Merchant Marine uniform, and a few photos of themselves. They also found boxes of their father's books and magazines and a pile of rejection slips. They learned that their father had submitted stories, mostly horror tales, to various magazines, but none had been accepted for publication. [22]

David and Stephen took some of the books and items home that day. They never found out what happened to the rest, because they mysteriously disappeared within a week, but Stephen had seen enough to realize that he shared more with his father than weak eyesight. His father loved horror tales and wrote his own. He bought and read horror books. In his father's collection were books by H. P. Lovecraft and other notable writers of fantasy and horror fiction. Stephen King loved horror all the more.

Stephen was constantly at the typewriter. He sold

some of his stories at school for a dime or a quarter. Then the teachers discovered that he was selling rewritten stories by other authors and stopped his business. His mother encouraged his writing and gave him stamps so he could submit his stories for publication. "You must not spend your life punching a time clock," she told her boys.[23] Stephen's stories were rejected, just like his father's, but he stuck to it. He refused to give up the way his father had.

He continued to worry about war with the Soviet Union. Nikita Khrushchev, premier of the Soviet Union, had taken off one of his shoes during a United Nations meeting, pounded it on his desk, and threatened to bury the United States. Although in 1958, the Soviet Union, Britain, and the United States had informally agreed to stop nuclear testing, the Soviet Union startled the world in 1961 when it tested a number of nuclear bombs. The United States and Britain resumed nuclear testing in 1962.

Stephen finished eighth grade in the spring of 1962. He had the best grades of all the graduates; however, there were only three students in his class. He was too young to get a job, so he spent the summer months writing fantasy, horror, and science fiction stories. At fourteen he was unable to fight the dreaded Soviets from the other side of the earth, but he could fight invading aliens from outer space.

Education and Rejection

Stephen King's personal world expanded in the fall of 1962. Instead of a rural one-room school, he attended a high school with dozens of rooms and as many teachers. Instead of walking a hundred yards to school, he took a limousine. It was an old one, rather beaten up, but the community hired the limo and its owner to transport nine students to the new high school in Lisbon Falls.

He had more space at home, too. His brother, David, had been accepted at the University of Maine and moved to Orono that fall, leaving the upstairs bedroom to Stephen. Neither boy wanted to share a room on weekends or for the summer, so David moved into a small downstairs room. The room was barely

Stephen and nine other rural students rode to Lisbon High School, above, in an old, beat-up limousine.

large enough for his twin bed, but it gave both boys a space of their own.

Stephen and his good friend Chris Chesley attended different high schools, so the boys saw each other only on weekends. They wasted little time talking about school. Instead, they read, wrote, and hitch-hiked into Lewiston to see horror movies at the Ritz.[1] Chris, unlike his friend, did not submit stories to fantasy and science fiction magazines, so he had no need for a big nail like the one that jutted out from the wall in Stephen's bedroom. The nail skewered the rejection slips Stephen had been collecting since he was twelve.

In 1963, sixteen-year-old Stephen and fourteen-year-old Chris self-published a second volume of *People, Places, and Things.* Four of the stories were "Hotel at the End of the Road," "The Stranger," "The Other Side of the Fog," and "Never Look Behind You." Once again they mimeographed each copy in the basement. Fewer than a dozen copies were printed and distributed, but it was a big step in fulfilling Stephen's dreams. He told his friend, "You know what I'm gonna do the first time I hit it big, Chris? I'm gonna get myself a great big Cadillac."[2]

Fears followed Stephen to high school. He worried that he would be unable to make friends. He was afraid of being afraid and not being able to tell anybody. He had a fear of not being good enough and a constant fear that he was alone. He covered up these fears by cracking jokes.[3]

Not all fears could be forgotten with a joke. Around this time, Stephen's grandmother became ill. One night, while his mother sat at his grandmother's bedside, Stephen was busy cooking dinner—hamburgers and fried potatoes. His mother came into the kitchen and said, "Stevie, I think she's passed, but I can't tell. Would you come and look?"[4] Stephen took a mirror from his mother's purse and held it to his grandmother's nose to check for breathing. When no fog formed on the mirror, Stephen informed his mother and Daddy Guy, who sat quietly in the corner, that Mama was dead. Daddy Guy died about a year later.

Another person whose death strongly affected Stephen was President John F. Kennedy. Stephen was in the limousine on his way home from school one November day in 1963 when the driver told him of the president's assassination. It scared him more than the announcement about *Sputnik 1* in the movie theater four years earlier.

Stephen had a B average in high school and was seldom in trouble. He was good, but not so good that he drew attention to himself, and he was never so bad that warning notices were sent home to his mother.[5] In fact, he considered himself a dud, just sort of a nerdy kid who did not get beaten up much because he was so big. Students said about him: "King—he's weird. Big glasses. Reads a lot. Big teeth."[6]

He played football, played guitar in a rock band, and joined the staff of the high school newspaper. In tenth grade, Stephen decided to self-publish a satire of the school paper. His *Village Vomit* poked fun at teachers by name. The school administrators were not happy with his publication. But instead of suspending him for three days, they got him a job with the town's newspaper so he would stay out of trouble. Stephen worked for the *Lisbon Enterprise*, earning a half cent per word for writing high school sports stories. This was the start of his professional training. He learned about deadlines, objective reporting, and rewriting.[7]

Money was always a problem for the Kings. The brothers found jobs as soon as they were old enough. David had worked for his high school on the janitorial staff. Stephen worked the three-to-eleven shift at the textile mill in Lisbon Falls. Getting home after work was often a problem. Seven miles was too far to walk that late at night, so sometimes he hitchhiked.

He was seventeen when he could finally afford a

car. He needed it not only to get home from work at night but also to avoid having to ride with the strange girl who sat silently in the back of the school limo, all alone. He bought his brother's Ford Galaxie for $250. The car was junk when David bought it and it had become worse. Still, it got Stephen to school, to work, and home again. After a couple of years, he replaced the Ford with a 1956 Plymouth he called Christine.[8]

The collection of rejection slips skewered on the nail in Stephen's bedroom kept growing, but he did not stop writing or publishing. In June 1964 he self-published *The Star Invaders*, a three-thousand-word science fiction thriller that included vivid images of the horrors of atomic energy.[9]

A year later, when he was eighteen, Stephen King received his first acceptance. His story, "I Was a Teenage Grave Robber," was about an orphaned boy who accepts a job as a grave robber for a scientist. It was published in a magazine called *Comic Review*. Twice the length of *The Star Invaders*, it was good enough to be reprinted in a revised form in *Stories of Suspense* two years later.[10] He did not receive any money, but now he could say that he was a professionally published author.

By the time Stephen graduated from high school, he had completed his first novel, *The Aftermath*. In his previous stories, threats had come from beyond planet Earth. In this fifty-thousand-word story, an atomic war destroys a large part of the world's population before aliens land and attempt to dominate Earth.

He started his second novel the summer after high

Stephen King's 1966 high school graduation picture. By then, he was already a writing machine, turning out newspaper articles, stories, and even a full-length novel.

school graduation. *Getting It On* was about the fear of not fitting in and was considered by critics to be his first mature work. Starting with this book, his stories would be about ordinary people in extraordinary circumstances.[11]

Drew University, a private Methodist college in Madison, New Jersey, accepted Stephen King after high school graduation, but even with his summer jobs he could not afford the tuition. Instead, he accepted a scholarship to attend the University of Maine at Orono. Ten thousand people lived in Orono in 1966, and King wrote, "Outside on the grass between Gannet and Androscoggin Hall there were more people playing football than there were in my home town."[12]

King put on his beanie (a cap worn by all first-year college men) and eased into college life. He once again shared a room, walked to classes, cracked jokes, and tried to fit in. He dressed in faded jeans and casual shirts. In the summer he wore sandals or went barefoot. He sometimes had a beard. Although he dressed like many others on campus, he still stood out. He was six feet, four inches tall, he wore thick glasses, and he read constantly, even in the cafeteria line.

As much as King liked writing, he did not enjoy all his writing classes. One creative writing professor insisted he analyze everything he wrote. That made writing work instead of pleasure, and King felt that his creativity suffered.[13]

King worked in the university library during the school year and continued to work at the textile mill when he was home during the summer. Between his freshman and sophomore years, he wrote a short story, "The Glass Floor," and submitted it to a publisher who had contributed many rejection slips to his nail. This time was different. King was paid $35, and his story appeared in *Startling Mystery Stories* in the fall of 1967. He got a lot of satisfaction from this sale. As he said later, "Someone had finally paid me some real money for what I found in my head."[14] The money he earned from "The Glass Floor" was welcome. While he was in college, his mother sometimes went without food to send him $5 each week.[15]

King never had enough money. He typed some of his stories on odd-sized, heavy green paper that he found in the library.[16] He called the collection *The Gunslinger* but put it away rather than submit it for publication.[17] Regardless of King's finances, he continued to write and submit short stories, fantasy/horror stories, science fiction stories, and novels to magazines and publishing houses. His first completed novel, *The Long Walk*, was sent to Random House's first-novel contest when King was twenty. He got another rejection slip.[18]

At times, King seemed to be the only one who thought he could make a living by writing. The English professors enjoyed King's verbal humor, but some thought his writing would come to nothing. After all, it was so different.[19]

The college literary magazine, *Ubris*, published two of King's short stories, "Here There Be Tygers" and "Cain Rose Up," in the spring of 1968. He made no money, but he did make an impression on other students. He was not an ordinary writer; he had a style of his own that people liked.

The university offered many literature courses but none about popular American fiction, the kind of books King read in the lunch line. He asked if he could teach a class; he knew a lot about the topic from all of the books he had read. Graduate students sometimes teach or assist a professor, but no under-graduate student had ever taught an English course at the University of Maine.[20] The English Department agreed that twenty-one-year-old Stephen King could teach a course called Popular Literature and Culture.

He continued to write stories for *Ubris* and joined the staff of *The Maine Campus*, the college newspaper. In his junior year, he started his own column called "King's Garbage Truck." Right from the beginning he showed that his interests were broad. His first column, published on February 20, 1969, reviewed a production put on by the Goddard College Dancers. The last half of his column gave a thumbs-up to the new movie *Hush . . . Hush, Sweet Charlotte*. He reviewed plays, such as *Romeo and Juliet* (2/27/69), and movies, such as *Doctor Zhivago* (4/10/69). Some of his columns were serious, like the one that expressed concern over a nominee for the University Board of Trustees (5/22/69). Others were humorous or were spoofs like his *Village Vomit* publication in high school. In one issue, King called himself the President Emeritus of the N.G.U.T.S.C.M.C (The Nitty Gritty Up Tight Society for a Campus With More Cools), demanded more courses like plumbing and fingernail growing, and said that if the university did not agree, he would start a campus strike (4/24/69). A year later he was writing about real student strikes and protests.

Political and social horrors continued while King was in college. Robert Kennedy, Dr. Martin Luther King, Jr., and four protesting students at Kent State University were killed. Young men were drafted to fight in Vietnam. Stephen King quit the Republican Party because President Nixon failed to stop the fighting. He wrote about these issues in "King's Garbage Truck," talked about them with fellow students, walked in protest lines, and attended rallies.

A record number of men attended college in the late sixties so they would not be drafted to fight in the Vietnam War. However, Stephen King had flat feet and very bad eyesight. Because of these physical conditions, he would not be called to serve in the military.[21]

The last "King's Garbage Truck" column, one of the shorter ones, announced his birth into the real world. He wrote it much like a birth announcement with his name, date of birth (graduation), age, weight, hair, and eye color. Then, on June 5, 1970, Stephen King accepted his diploma and, with a state teaching certificate, left the protective walls of the university.

A Breakthrough Sale

Teaching jobs were hard to find in 1970, so Stephen King found work wherever he could. His first job was pumping gas for $1.25 an hour. Then he started working full-time for the New Franklin Laundry in Bangor. He made $60 a week running an industrial washing machine and ironing sheets in a room that was hot, steamy, and noisy.[1] A responsible worker, he got to work on time, did his job well, and got along with the staff. Whenever he had a story published, he brought it in to show to the other workers. He did not brag about his writing success; he just enjoyed sharing it.[2] These stories paid about $250 each, about the same as his monthly salary.

King lived in Bangor, Maine, with his good friend Chris Chesley, who hitchhiked back and forth to the

As one of his first jobs, King ran an industrial washing machine and ironed sheets at the New Franklin Laundry.

university in Orono.[3] Between his job and his writing, King spent time with Tabitha Spruce, a coworker from the university library whom he had started dating before graduation. Spruce was a history major who also had dreams of writing. They married on January 2, 1971, in Old Town, Maine, Spruce's childhood home. King said years later, "The only important thing I ever did in my life for a conscious reason was to ask Tabitha Spruce . . . if she would marry me."[4]

They rented a double-wide mobile home, which King called their trailer, on a lot in Herman, Maine. Chris Chesley rented a room from them to help the

Kings pay their bills. Tabitha King finished her degree in May 1971 and had no more luck finding a job than her husband. She ended up working as a waitress for a Dunkin' Donuts shop in Bangor. The two never had enough money. Often King sold a story just in time to pay the phone bill, repair the car, or pay the rent.

Fortunately, King found a teaching job before their first child, Naomi, was born. Two years earlier, Hampden Academy had requested that King shave his beard and get a haircut before taking him on as a student teacher.[5] King had grumbled but did as they asked. Now Hampden Academy offered him a full-time teaching job. He taught seven classes of English and supervised one period of study hall. His office seemed appropriate for a horror writer—it overlooked a cemetery.

Students enjoyed King's English classes. He wanted them to have fun writing. He taught classics like the novel *Dracula* by Bram Stoker and the play *Our Town* by Thorton Wilder.[6] King was easygoing with his students, but at the same time he was watching them closely, committing their habits to memory. Then, in the evening, he wrote stories about similar teenagers.

King's salary, a respectable $6,400 a year, was still not enough to pay off student loans and support a family. He now had the added responsibility of providing for his mother, who still lived in Durham. She was suffering from cancer and could no longer work, so the Kings regularly sent her money.

King cleared enough space in the furnace room of the trailer to set up a home office. He found a discarded fourth-grade desk that he balanced on his lap, and using his wife's old typewriter, he wrote for about an hour and a half each night.[7] He decorated a wall of the furnace room with a dart board. He pinned his rejection slips to it and sometimes threw darts at them when he felt discouraged.[8]

The monsters in King's writing no longer came from afar, like the dinosaur in his first story or the aliens in *The Star Invaders*. He had learned by watching Alfred Hitchcock movies and *The Twilight Zone*, a popular weekly TV show, that the scariest monsters live among the ordinary population. He finished *Getting It On*, the novel he started the summer before college, and sent it off to Doubleday Publishers. Editor Bill Thompson took an interest in the book and worked with King on a number of revisions. But Thompson was unable to persuade the rest of the publishing team to offer twenty-four-year-old Stephen King a contract.[9] King put the manuscript back into his writing trunk.

With money tight, King could not take the summer off as many teachers do. He went back to work at the laundry and continued writing at night. King sent Bill Thompson at Doubleday several other manuscripts. They were rejected without the encouragement that *Getting It On* had received. King put them away, too.[10]

Meanwhile, Tabitha King was pregnant with their son Joseph, and King felt more pressure than ever to provide for his family. Repairs to their car had been put off so long that it barely ran. They had no phone.

Occasionally, King sold a story to a magazine, but that money often bought medicine or another necessity. He knew that big money would come from

While his students studied English at the Hampden Academy, above, Stephen King studied the students. Then he wrote stories featuring similar teens.

novels, not short stories. Even so, King started a new short story he called "Carrie." It was about a high school girl who did not fit in, like the lonely girl in the back of the limousine the students took back and forth to Lisbon High School. Carrie's mother always quoted the Bible, much like one of King's coworkers at the laundry. Much of the plot was based on King's experiences as a high school teacher. But he had trouble writing from the female perspective, got discouraged, and threw the story away. His wife retrieved the manuscript from the trash, read it, and told him it had great possibilities. She persuaded him to turn it into a novel and helped him with some of the details about women and their unique problems.[11]

By March 1973, *Carrie* had been revised with the help of Bill Thompson at Doubleday, but it had not been accepted for publication. The Kings still had no telephone and Chris Chesley still rented a room from them. Stephen King still had hopes of making it as a writer, but hope was dwindling. Sixty short stories and four novels had been rejected.[12]

Several horror movies were popular about that time: *Rosemary's Baby, The Exorcist,* and *The Other.* Thompson thought *Carrie* had the same appeal and worked hard to convince the staff of Doubleday that it was worth publishing. He managed to get a number of people interested, so he invited King to New York for a publisher's lunch to discuss the book. Thompson did not realize at the time what King would have to do to get to that lunch.

Stephen King borrowed enough money from his wife's grandmother to buy new shoes and a

Greyhound bus ticket from Bangor to New York City and back. He wore a corduroy jacket and his best and only sweater, a bulky red turtleneck. After a sleepless night on the bus, he arrived in New York at six in the morning. His appointment was for noon. He spent a couple of hungry hours in the bus terminal before walking to the Doubleday offices. King had never seen tall buildings like those in New York City. He kept looking up to see the tops of them, and by the time he got to Doubleday his neck hurt. In addition, his new shoes had rubbed painful blisters on his feet.[13] The receptionist announced him right away.

"I went out to greet him," Bill Thompson said. "This giant of a man was looming there. I'm six-foot-two and he made me feel small. He was also very hairy, with a beard that clearly lived a life of its own; so did his smile and his handshake. Stephen King had come to town."[14]

Lunch included drinks, and King had two of them on an empty stomach. This made him almost drunk. Then, part of his pasta lunch clung to his beard even after he had finished his meal. Fortunately, King was there to make an impression as a writer, not as a neat eater. After lunch Thompson told him that *Carrie* had a good chance of being published, and he would keep promoting it. King had come all the way from Bangor just to hear those words. He was back home that night.[15]

Thompson managed to convince Doubleday to publish *Carrie*. He also managed to get more money in advance. He sent King a telegram that read, "Carrie

Officially a Doubleday Book. $2,500 Advance Against Royalties. Congrats, Kid—The Future Lies Ahead. Bill."[16]

The telegram meant that after King signed the contract, Doubleday would send him $2,500. He would also receive royalties, a percentage of the profit from book sales. Every time somebody bought a copy of *Carrie*, King would get paid a small amount.

It was an ordinary March day at the Kings' trailer. As usual, Chesley was at the university, and Stephen King was teaching school. Tabitha King was at home with Naomi and baby Joseph when the telegram arrived. She ran next door to phone her husband. A year earlier, she had rescued *Carrie* from the trash; now she could announce its sale.[17]

When King got home that afternoon, Chesley watched the children while Tabitha and Stephen King talked and cried.[18] Soon after, the King family moved into an apartment in Bangor, junked their car, bought a blue Ford Pinto, and had a phone installed. Now writing two hours a day, seven days a week, King was averaging six pages a day.[19]

While Stephen was teaching *Dracula* to his high school English class, Tabitha King told him she wondered what would happen if Dracula came to a small town in Maine.[20] She argued that everyone would know, but her husband doubted they would. He began working on the story: A vampire named Barlow moves to a small town in Maine, and strange things start happening.

On Mother's Day two months after his telegram, Thompson phoned King with more good news. Doubleday did not publish paperback books, so the company sold the rights to print *Carrie* in paperback to New American Library (NAL) for $400,000. King would get half of that.[21] He was stunned. He called Thompson back immediately and asked if he really meant $40,000. The editor repeated $400,000. The first thing King thought of was getting his wife a present. It was Sunday, and everything was closed except a drugstore. After wandering up and down the aisles, he bought a hair dryer. The next day he gave her a better present—he told her that they were going to retire and become full-time writers.[22]

King finished the school year and packed up his belongings. No more planning lessons or correcting other people's writing. No outside obligations to keep him from what he liked doing most. He said good-bye to the students who had enjoyed his teaching, to the other teachers who had become his friends, and to his principal, who thought he had promise as a teacher.[23] For King, teaching high school was now history.

6

A Growing Reputation

The King family packed up their household in the summer of 1973 and moved to North Windham, Maine, a small town near Sebago Lake. It was the perfect place to write.[1] King fished in the lake. The family picnicked in the woods and visited friends and relatives around Durham, just twenty miles away. King's brother, David, had been a math teacher but now worked for the city of Mexico, Maine, only an hour north of Sebago Lake. David and his wife, Linda, had married soon after college. The two families would get together and Naomi and Joe would play with David's two daughters, Karen and Katherine.

As soon as King finished *Second Coming*, his story about the vampire Barlow in Maine, he sent it off to Bill Thompson. The editor worried that King would be considered strictly a horror writer unless he wrote something different, but King just wanted to write what came to mind, whether or not it was horror. Once again Thompson worked closely with King, helping him revise the manuscript twice before it was accepted and renamed *'Salem's Lot.*

Then, on December 18, 1973, King's mother, Nellie Ruth King, died in Mexico, Maine. She was only sixty years old and had suffered painfully with cancer for a year and a half. She lived just long enough to see her son—the boy she nurtured with classic comic books and horror tales—begin a successful writing career.

King reacted to his mother's death by writing a new book about a man who loses his son to cancer. As horrible as cancer and death might be, *Roadwork* was not a horror story but a serious novel that helped him deal with his grief. He wrote it in six weeks, then put it in his writing trunk for a few years.

Before *Carrie* was released on April 5, 1974, Thompson sent out advance copies and a letter to booksellers, describing *Carrie* as a tremendously readable thriller that might be the novel of the year. "Don't start it unless the evening in front of you is free of appointments; this one is a cooker," he wrote.[2]

Carrie received mostly good reviews as a fantasy/ horror story. Not every reviewer liked it, but one who did was Burton Hatlen, King's composition professor. Hatlen believed King had the promise of becoming a major American writer.[3]

Doubleday published thirty thousand copies of *Carrie.* The company had counted on prepublication advertising to attract buyers. The back cover of the book told potential readers nothing about the plot, the characters, or any of the supernatural happenings in the story. Readers bought it anyway.

The same month *Carrie* came out, Thompson decided to publish *'Salem's Lot*. Almost immediately, New American Library purchased paperback rights for $500,000, and King received half.[4]

King now wrote four hours each day, every day of the week. He took off three days a year: his birthday, Christmas, and the Fourth of July.[5] He still used a typewriter and did the typing himself. He started his books not knowing for sure how they would end. Planning plots, he thought, closed him off from any interesting side trip that might come along.[6] The first draft of any of King's books was the story as it came into his head. The second time through, he checked his facts and rewrote to please his editor. In the third draft, he concentrated on language, so the words and sentences would balance and interest the reader.[7]

In the afternoons, he handled his own correspondence, updated his appointment calendar, and made phone calls. He was not yet rich and famous. He could not afford a secretary.

Since the Kings still rented their home, and their children were not yet in school, the family was free to travel. King could not remember ever living outside Maine, where all of his stories took place, and he was ready to change settings. In late summer 1974, the family moved to Boulder, Colorado. It had the advantages of a city without being too large and crowded, and it was convenient to all sorts of outdoor recreation. But that is not why the Kings decided to relocate there.

"The only important thing I ever did in my life for a conscious reason," says Stephen King, "was to ask Tabitha [above] . . . to marry me."

When his wife asked where he wanted to move, King had no idea. So she opened a map of the United States, tied a handkerchief over his eyes, and told him to point. He pointed to Boulder, Colorado.[8] The nearby Rocky Mountains inspired his first hardback best-seller.

King started two novels in the fall of 1974. One was left unfinished. The other was about a boy who was psychic and could foretell the future. He and his family were cut off from the rest of the world in a place where nightmares turned real. Neither story seemed to develop very well. Then Tabitha and Stephen King spent the night at the Stanley Hotel in Estes Park.

Everything King experienced at the hotel came together at the right time. What if the wind had been calm instead of fierce? What if other guests had been around to socialize with? What if he had lacked the cash to pay the bill? Without any one of these events, *The Shining* may never have been written.

When the couple got back to Boulder, King rented an office downtown so he could write undisturbed by the busy household and chattering toddlers. He never saw the landlord; he just left the rent payment beside the coffeepot each week, and the money was gone the next day.[9] He worked undisturbed for an intense six weeks until the first draft of *The Shining* was finished.

In January 1975 King went to New York to meet with Thompson. They had a casual lunch at a little hamburger place. It was a much more comfortable lunch than the first one they had shared. The purpose of the meeting was to go over *'Salem's Lot*, which was scheduled to be published in October. King took the opportunity to tell Thompson about *The Shining*. Once again Thompson warned him that he might be stereotyped as a horror writer.[10] That was fine with King. He returned to Colorado and put the finishing touches on his story.

Always concerned about frightful or tragic events in real life, King was haunted by news of an accident involving a chemical spill in Utah. The wind was blowing away from the nearby town, so no people died from the poison, but many sheep did. King asked himself, what if something started killing off the entire population? Instead of chemicals, he decided a super-flu would destroy almost all of civilization. His novel *The Stand*, which took two years to write, ended up being twelve hundred pages long and weighing twelve pounds. Not a traditional horror story, *The Stand* is a mixture of science fiction and fantasy. After the flu, a small population of good people confronts an aggressive group of evil personalities.

After a year in Boulder, the Kings moved back to Maine and bought a home on the west side of Long Lake in Bridgton. *Carrie* had sold over one million copies by then, and King had many fans. They wrote him, visited Bridgton, talked to local people about him, and took pictures of his house. When his second book, *'Salem's Lot*, appeared in print in October 1975, King was twenty-eight and rapidly becoming a popular author.

The movie industry had showed an interest in producing *Carrie* even before it appeared in print. The resulting film starred Sissy Spacek as Carrie. Two other actors in the film who later became well known were Amy Irving and John Travolta. Shooting started in spring 1976, two years after the book was released.

After the film opened, King received invitations from reporters, schools, clubs, and service organizations for interviews and appearances. He already had a full schedule; he was sorry that he had to say no to the requests. After all, these were the people who bought his books and made him rich. When he turned down an invitation, King wondered if people thought, "That stuck-up big-shot writer."[11] But King needed to use his time to write and provide readers with the books they wanted so much to read.

Doubleday published *The Shining* in January 1977. *The Shining* was the first of King's books to make *The New York Times* best-seller list. Other writers started imitating King's style.[12] Filmmaker Stanley Kubrick, who directed *2001: A Space Odyssey*, was interested in making the movie version.

Doubleday would publish only two more Stephen King books: *The Stand*, King's story about the super-flu and its effects on civilization, and *Night Shift*, a collection of his short stories, including "The Lawnmower Man" and "Children of the Corn." Although King and Thompson enjoyed a good publishing relationship, King did not like some of the details of Doubleday's contract.[13]

At a New York literary party in 1976, King had met Kirby McCauley, a literary agent who represented several writers in the science fiction and fantasy field. King and McCauley started corresponding, and eventually King decided to have McCauley represent him.

McCauley handled the business aspects of the contract between King and his publishers, negotiating advances, royalties, and film and paperback rights.

Since Doubleday first published *Carrie* in 1974, more than 6 million copies had been sold, an unbelievable number for a writer who had published so little. Now King had a new contract with New American Library to write three new books: *The Dead Zone, Firestarter*, and a third novel to be decided.[14]

7

A Maine Writer

In September 1977, New American Library published *Rage*, a paperback book by Richard Bachman. Who was Richard Bachman? The picture on the dust jacket was of Richard Manuel, an old friend of Stephen King's literary agent, Kirby McCauley. Fans wanting to meet Richard Bachman found it impossible. Bachman claimed to be a chicken farmer from New Hampshire whose face was said to be disfigured by cancer. He was too shy for interviews or appearances.[1] Who was the real author of *Rage*? Stephen King. Why would a famous writer use a pen name?

Many publishers preferred to publish only one book each year for a writer under contract. Fans waited impatiently for a new book to hit the stores, then bought it, read it, and waited impatiently for the next one. If a writer came out with two books in one year, publishers thought the sale of one book might hurt the sale of the other.

King had a trunk full of unpublished stories and novels. Some had already been rejected; others had never been submitted. *Rage* had been put in the trunk soon after King's high school graduation. Originally titled *Getting It On*, it was the novel Bill Thompson had taken a liking to but eventually rejected.[2]

By 1977, the popularity of science fiction, fantasy, and horror had grown enormously. Stephen King dug out *Getting It On*, renamed it *Rage*, and New American Library published it under the Bachman name. *Publishers Weekly* gave it a weak review, saying, "Even a lesson in Latin grammar would have been more involving. . . ."[3] But people bought it.

About the time *Rage* appeared in print, the Kings decided to sell their Bridgton home and move to England for a year. Each move had provided King with new settings, new material, and new horrors. He put an ad in the *Fleet News*, an English newspaper, that read, "Wanted, a draughty Victorian house in the country with dark attic and creaking floorboards, preferably haunted."[4] The Kings rented Mourlands, a house in Fleet, Hants. It was not haunted but it was large enough for the family of five, which now included seven-month-old Owen.

Naomi and Joe King attended St. Nicholas School while their dad started work on an English ghost story. King decided this would be the third book in his contract with NAL.[5] The ghost in this story never made it onto paper, but a savage Saint Bernard dog did.

King had read a tragic story in the Portland, Maine, newspaper about a boy who was attacked and killed by a Saint Bernard. King's mind flashed back to his own experience with a Saint Bernard a couple of years before. He had taken his motorcycle to a garage for repairs. As he parked the cycle, a very large dog marched across the road straight toward him. The dog growled and looked as if it would attack. The owner looked at King and said, "Joe must not like you."[6] King was thinking the same thing, and his fear of being attacked by the dog was never forgotten. Now, living in the English countryside, King started his next book, *Cujo*, which was set in Maine. What if a rabid Saint Bernard terrorized a mother and son trapped in a broken-down Ford Pinto? It was a place, and a car, he knew well.

Peter Straub, an American writer of supernatural books, lived nearby in England. One evening, the Kings joined the Straubs for dinner. After dinner, the two men discussed writing a story together.[7] Each admired the other's talents. They agreed that not only would they enjoy writing the story, their fans would enjoy reading it. It would be almost seven years before their work would reach the public.

King did not write the expected ghost story, but after three months in England, the first draft of *Cujo* was finished, and the family moved back to Maine in December 1977. They bought a house in Center Lovell, a small town on Kezar Lake near the New Hampshire border.

In 1978 Doubleday published the fourth and fifth

of King's books. *Night Shift*, his collection of short stories, came out in February. *The Stand* was released in September, but King was unhappy with it. Doubleday thought that twelve hundred pages was too long and had King cut out four hundred pages. Instead of throwing them out, King put them in his trunk.[8]

The Kings lived in their new house only a few months before moving again. An English professor at the University of Maine retired in 1975, leaving a position open for a creative writing teacher. Instead of hiring a professor full-time, the university decided to invite well-known writers to teach for short periods. Stephen King rented a house in Orrington, just outside Bangor, so he could be the creative writing instructor for the 1978–1979 school year.

King had an office and a hundred students in each of four courses: creative writing, poetry, and two literature classes. One course used films for instruction. Students evaluated *Psycho, The Exorcist, Invasion of the Body Snatchers,* and others, but not *Carrie.* He could not locate a copy.[9] King was so popular with students and faculty that the university asked him to extend his appointment. He refused.[10] He had a multitude of ideas to turn into books.

Bill Thompson, now a senior editor at Everest House, suggested that King write a nonfiction book about the history of horror in books, movies, radio, and TV. King titled the book *Danse Macabre* and included autobiographical material. Writing nonfiction required a different strategy from writing fiction. When writing fiction, King wrote the story first, and then he made sure facts supported his story. In nonfiction,

For Stephen King, here at his desk in his tower office, stories lurk in every experience.

facts were more important. Every statement had to be researched and supported. *Danse Macabre* took him two years to write, but he had other stories developing at the same time.

The idea for his next fantasy/horror novel came from an unfortunate family experience. Naomi's cat, Smucky, was run over by a car on Thanksgiving Day, 1979. Naomi was extremely upset, so the family decided on a proper burial for the cat. The neighborhood children had claimed a piece of land in the nearby woods as a cemetery for their pets. Tall trees protected graves from the sun in the summer, and colorful leaves decorated the ground in the autumn. Smucky was buried here with other beloved pets. The children's sign read, "Pets Sematary."

After the burial, King's first thought—what if a cat came back to life?—was quickly followed by a second thought: What if a human came back to life? *Pet Sematary* was started soon after the cat's funeral, and the first draft was finished by May 1980. King decided it was too frightening even for readers of horror, so he put it aside to be revised and published at a later date.[11]

The family moved back to their home in Center Lovell, where King continued to write. In July, the second Richard Bachman book hit the shelves. *The Long Walk*, a book King had written during college and submitted to a first-novel competition, is about one hundred boys who start walking in northern Maine. They walk until just one is left. Everyone has the same goal and the same opportunity, but only one survives. The paperback book was published by NAL and sold alongside *Rage*, the first Bachman book. Richard Bachman was not yet a well-known writer, and King was not worried that his pen name would become more popular than his own.

A month after *The Long Walk*, Viking published the first of its King books. In spite of its title, *The Dead Zone* is more of a romantic thriller than a horror book. The dead zone refers to a damaged part of Johnny Smith's brain, the area necessary for language and visualization skills. Johnny has been injured in a hockey accident. Coincidentally, another part of Johnny's brain has been overstimulated and has given him telepathic skills, which he does not know how to use.

Viking sent King on an author's tour to promote *The Dead Zone*. He visited bookstores in seven major cities in six days and said he was so tired, he felt as if he had been in a pillow fight.

King loved baseball and attended Boston Red Sox games whenever he could. Sometimes when he was in New York City, he had business meetings at Yankee Stadium, mixing business with pleasure. Part of King lived and died with the baseball season. On the first day of spring training he shaved off his beard. He stayed clean-shaven until the last day of the World Series.[12] Then he would grow his beard again. Photos of King were a clue to what time of year they were taken. A beard meant autumn or winter. No beard meant baseball season.

King's next book for Viking was *Christine*. It was named for a car—a 1958 Plymouth Fury—that turns out to be haunted. King also finished *Danse Macabre*, the nonfiction book about the horror genre, and wrote some short stories and his first screenplay, *Creepshow*. One story, "The Mist," became one of his most popular creations. It was first printed in *Dark Forces*, a horror anthology compiled by Kirby McCauley.

By the end of 1979, Stephen King, just thirty-two years old, had eight novels on bookstore shelves, two with Bachman's name. *Danse Macabre* and *Christine* were ready for publication, and his first screenplay, *Creepshow*, was ready for production. One movie, *Carrie*, had been released, and another, *The Shining*, was in production. In November, King's first made-for-TV movie, *'Salem's Lot*, aired in two parts.

King traveled a lot, and he met frequently with publishers and producers. In 1978 he served as a judge for the World Fantasy Awards, which honors exceptional authors writing fantasy, science fiction, and horror. A year later he attended the awards as a nominee for *Night Shift* (in the best collection/anthology category) and for *The Stand* (best novel category). He did not win in 1979, but he drew a great deal of attention to himself and became one of the people to know in the fantasy/horror field.

Stephen King at the World Fantasy Awards was like a kid in a candy shop. Many talented writers attended, giving King access to many new ideas. King stayed up late discussing trends. He autographed books, gave speeches, and enjoyed himself. He had bodyguards to keep fans at a distance, so he could participate in the activities. Stephen King's popularity as a fantasy/horror writer had skyrocketed.

Stephen King's books sell an astounding number of copies.

Writing in a
Haunted House

Ghosts. Stephen King had hoped ghosts would haunt his rented house in England, but he never saw or felt one. In 1980, the Kings bought a 129-year-old house in Bangor, Maine. It had twenty-three rooms, two towers, secret passages, and a ghost.

The Kings knew nothing about the ghost until after they moved in. Everyone in the family felt an odd sensation when entering the living room. Even the pets shied away from that corner of the house. The room was redecorated with a new rug and fresh wallpaper, but people and pets still felt uncomfortable.[1] Finally, the Kings decided that the rumored ghost must live there. Eventually, the ghost stopped haunting them, or they just got used to the feeling.

Moving into this house was a dream come true for Tabitha King. As a teenager, she had walked up and down West Broadway looking at the mansions. One house always caught her eye. It had two towers and a large front porch with pillars supporting a balcony. The house was built in 1857 and was the first house on West Broadway, now called the historic district. It happened to be for sale just when the Kings were looking for a home to settle into.

The house was perfect for them, and Bangor was the perfect town. The town offered good schools and libraries, bookstores and department stores, movie theaters, and a pretty setting along the Penobscot River. King felt comfortable because Bangor men usually wore jeans and work shirts. In Bangor—which called itself Paul Bunyan country and the lumber capital of the world—King could eat hamburgers at the local McDonald's, shop in his favorite bookstore, or watch his children's baseball games without being disturbed. Bangor treated him and his family like any other residents.[2]

Fans kept knocking on his door, so King had a hand-forged iron fence built to surround the house. The 270-foot fence took a year and a half to build and weighed eleven thousand pounds. The two gates leading up to the front door are decorated with spiders, spiderwebs, goat heads, and winged bats. A three-headed griffin guards the driveway. Tourists still flock to King's home to take pictures, but the fence keeps fans from knocking on his door.

When they moved, King decided his manuscripts should also have a new home. He had old drafts of

Carrie, The Dead Zone, The Stand, and *The Shining,* proofs from the publisher, and correspondence with editors. Six boxes of his work went to the Fogler Library at the University of Maine, Orono, the same library where Stephen and Tabitha King had worked during college.

King no longer traveled around looking for new settings and ideas. He stayed at home and created Castle Rock, Maine, a setting for many of his stories.

A second Viking book, *Firestarter,* came out in September 1980. It has a political theme—the effects of government on people's lives—and deals with *pyrokinetic powers*, a term King invented to describe the mental ability to start fires.

At the World Fantasy Awards in 1980, King was recognized for his special contributions to the field of fantasy writing. The award was a small bust of H. P. Lovecraft, a writer whose work King had admired since first finding a Lovecraft book among his father's possessions.

Director Stanley Kubrick's film version of *The Shining* came out in 1980. It was not a big hit. Kubrick had changed the story somewhat, so true King fans were disappointed. In addition, the movie ran somewhat long, two hours and fifteen minutes.

Meanwhile King's wife was having difficulty finding time to write with three children around the house. King bought her a new typewriter and told her to get an office. She did, and in 1981 her first novel, *Small World,* a political romance, was published by Macmillan. Many of Tabitha King's novels take place in Nodd's Ridge, a fictional town like Castle Rock. She

This statue of Paul Bunyan stands in Bangor, Maine, which once called itself the lumber capital of the world. After many years of moving around, the Kings settled happily into this comfortable Maine community.

has reported that there was no competition between her and her husband because they wrote on entirely different themes. She critiqued his work and has jokingly accused him of stealing her ideas.[3]

Even during vacations, King wrote. In February 1981, the family went to Puerto Rico. King took a manuscript he was working on, but he failed to produce what he wanted. Once again, the work grew much longer than he expected. Nevertheless, the publisher was delighted and printed *Cycle of the Werewolf* as a limited-edition book available by special order only.

Three new Stephen King books were published in 1981: *Roadwork*, the book written after his mother's death, with Richard Bachman listed as the author; *Cujo*, the novel about the rabid Saint Bernard; and *Danse Macabre*, King's nonfiction book about horror literature.

The following year *Different Seasons*, four short novels, and *The Running Man*, the fourth Richard Bachman book, hit the bookstores. King was featured in a television commercial for American Express. He was flattered by the attention. Stephen King was thirty-five years old, and now his face as well as his name was known throughout the world.

King's screenplay, *Creepshow*, was also produced in 1982. *Creepshow* is about a young boy who is caught reading a horror comic. His father throws the book outside, and the characters come to life. Stephen King made his big-screen acting debut in this movie. He played Jordy Verrill, not a major role but one that required a lot of makeup. Near the end of the shooting, King sat for six hours having fibrous globs glued to his body.[4] His son Joe also appeared in the film. Joe's costume consisted of a pair of pajamas, and he stayed in bed. His makeup was more realistic; he had a large bruise painted on his cheek. One night King and his son stopped at a McDonald's on the way home from shooting the film, and a crowd gathered to see the bruised kid in pajamas.[5]

One segment of *Creepshow* needed three thousand huge cockroaches. They were collected from large bat caves in South America. The Museum of Natural History in New York provided roach wranglers to care for the cockroaches, which lived in big garbage cans and ate dog chow and bananas.[6]

When he was in college, King had a 1956 Plymouth he named *Christine*. In 1983 Viking published *Christine*, the story of a 1958 red-and-white Plymouth Fury that had a mind of its own. Also in 1983, Doubleday printed and sold 657,000 copies of *Pet Sematary*, the frightening story King had written in 1978 after the family cat's funeral. Three films from King's works were released that year: *Cujo, The Dead Zone,* and *Christine.*

Over the years, King has received many distinguished awards. In 1980, *People* magazine named him Writer of the Year. In 1981, he received a special British Fantasy Award, a Career Alumni Award from the University of Maine, a World Fantasy Award nomination for "The Mist," and a best short story nomination. In 1982, *Cujo* won a British Fantasy Award, *Danse Macabre* won the Hugo Award in nonfiction,

A young Drew Barrymore, above with Stephen King, starred in the film version of King's novel Firestarter.

and "Do the Dead Sing?" won a World Fantasy Award for best short story.

Naomi King had never liked reading her father's horror stories, so in 1983 he wrote *Eyes of the Dragon*, a fantasy story with princes, castles, wizards, and dragons. Naomi loved it. King self-published the book a year later. His publishing company, called Philtrum Press, used state-of-the art printing equipment, not a typewriter that needed the "n"s filled in or a hand-cranked mimeograph machine. King published 1,250 copies. He gave 250 books as Christmas presents. The other thousand were sold through a lottery. These books are now expensive collector's items.[7]

By 1983, King had a secretary, a business manager, a lawyer, and an agent. Sometimes bodyguards and other support personnel were needed to help with his growing business. A two-hour book signing often turned out to be six hours long.[8] King was thirty-six years old and was one of the most popular writers in the world.

King still turned down invitations for appearances, but occasionally, he made an exception. In April 1983, he spoke at a fund-raiser for the public library in Billerica, Massachusetts. King entertained the audience for two hours by talking, reading stories, and answering questions.

Seven months later he was in Truth or Consequences, New Mexico, where the citizens provided an entertaining and busy day. Chris Chesley, King's longtime friend, and his wife, Lois, lived nearby. King had sent Chesley a copy of each of his books as it was published, but when he forgot to send a copy of *Different Seasons*, Lois Chesley went to the library to check out a copy. The librarian suggested she ask Stephen King if he would give a talk at their library. King agreed, and although he pleased hundreds of people, some left unhappy: King developed blisters on his fingers from signing autographs and was forced to stop before all his fans had their books signed.[9]

Stephen King was always a fan of rock music, and when Bangor station WACZ went up for sale in 1983, King bought it. He renamed it WZON, reminiscent of *The Twilight Zone* and his book *The Dead Zone*. The deejays chanted, "You're in the rock zone."[10] King could listen to the kind of music he liked any time he wanted. He seldom went to the station; he let the professionals do their job without his interference just as long as they played the music he enjoyed.[11]

Finally, in 1984, seven years after it was discussed in England, *The Talisman*, King's book with Peter Straub, was published. Fans of the two popular authors analyzed the book, trying to figure out who wrote which part. It had truly been a cooperative effort. Chapters traveled back and forth across the Atlantic for revisions until neither writer's style dominated the story.

Also in 1984, *The Dark Tower: Gunslinger*—the book originally written on green paper from the university library—was published by Donald M. Grant, Publisher, a small press in Rhode Island. King anticipated that *The Dark Tower* series would include seven titles.

Stephanie Spruce Leonard, Tabitha King's sister,

Hand-forged iron spiders and bats help give celebrity Stephen King some privacy from his fans.

had worked as King's secretary for several years, and in 1984 she suggested writing a monthly publication to let fans know what the author was doing. King agreed as long as he had nothing to do with it. With Stephanie Leonard as editor, the first edition of "Castle Rock"—named after King's fictional town— was issued in January 1985. Five hundred copies went out to fans that month. By July, circulation was 5,500. The newsletter, which averaged eight pages, answered questions about the writer, gave publishing information, and printed reviews and interviews. Sara Spruce, Tabitha's mother, handled the subscriptions, and Chris Spruce, Tabitha's brother, was the managing editor and did the layout and design.

Castle Rock was used as the setting for many of King's stories. "The Body," one of the four short novels in *Different Seasons*, was set in Castle Rock, but when director Rob Reiner made the movie, he changed the location to Castle Rock, Oregon. Called *Stand by Me*, the movie was filmed near Eugene, Oregon, but referred to places and things in Maine: Shiloh Church, the town of Durham, leeches in the river, a good friend named Chris who attended a different high school, and other incidents from King's childhood. In the movie, four boys—who are the same age as King when he saw the dead body by the pond— search the countryside to find the body of a boy who had been killed by a train. They want to become famous, but when they find the missing boy, they just stare, say a prayer, and go home. The movie was what is known as a sleeper—ticket sales started out slowly but then the film became very popular.

In 1985 King finished a screenplay called *Trucks*. Since his involvement in *Creepshow*, King felt comfortable around movie sets, so he decided to direct the film himself. Renamed *Maximum Overdrive*, it was filmed in Wilmington, North Carolina, between July and October 1985. King worked long hours six days a week, rode his motorcycle to and from the set, ate at McDonald's and other fast-food restaurants, and slept very little. He did not like directing the movie at all. "I had to work. I wasn't used to working. I hadn't worked in twelve years," he said. After finishing the film, King said that he had achieved his goal of making a "moron movie."[12] *Maximum Overdrive* was not a success in theaters, and King decided he would never do anything like that again until his children grew up. He disliked being away from home for that long.[13]

Stephen King liked working at home. It kept him close to his wife and children. He spent a lot of time parenting. He made breakfast for his children, supported their baseball teams, and encouraged them with their personal goals. He also gave them jobs. King's novels were now available on audiotape for the blind or for anyone who had no time to read but could listen while traveling or exercising. King hired his children to record books for him to listen to while in the car. Owen recorded detective novels, and Naomi recorded John Steinbeck stories.[14]

Stephen King moved his office from the main house to the second-floor room in the barn, which housed the indoor pool. He neither needed nor wanted the peace and quiet of the house—he usually played loud rock music while writing and disturbed

Stephen King's house is guarded by a three-headed griffin, a mythical beast.

the household. Once again, King had his children around him as he wrote. He watched them play in the pool and invited them into his office to chat.[15]

In 1985 the fifth Richard Bachman book, *Thinner*, was published. The main character, a lawyer, becomes thinner and thinner. One day his pants fall down while he is giving a speech in court. *Thinner* was received very differently from the other Bachman books. By now, several professional reviewers had decided that Richard Bachman was really Stephen King. On February 9, 1985, the *Bangor Daily News* officially revealed that King and Bachman were the same person. A humorous obituary read: "Richard Bachman—born in 1942, a graduate of the University of New Hampshire, a Vietnam veteran, window washer, commercial fisherman, private security guard, and most recently a dairy farmer and part-time writer— died a sudden death of what King termed 'cancer of the pseudonym' on January 9, 1985."[16]

Suddenly, there was an urgent need for Bachman books in bookstores. Only two were currently in print, *The Running Man* and *Thinner*, and King fans demanded them. *Thinner* became number one on the *Publishers Weekly* hardcover best-seller list.

Fans were suspicious that King might have used other pseudonyms. In the April 1985 issue of "Castle Rock," Stephanie Leonard admitted that King had once used the name John Swithen on a short story published in 1972. She assured readers that he had no other pen names.[17]

In 1985, *Silver Bullet*, a movie based on King's story *Cycle of the Werewolf*, and *Skeleton Crew*, a collection of short stories, came out. In October 1986, *It*—a story about a poor boy from Maine who wants to be a writer—was published. The book had taken five years to write. Orders were so numerous that *It* made the best-seller list even before the book was published. The following year four King books were published: *The Dark Tower II: The Drawing of the Three*; a new version of *The Eyes of the Dragon,* Naomi's fantasy; *Misery,* a thriller about a writer who is terrorized by a fanatical fan; and *The Tommyknockers,* about dead aliens found in a crashed spaceship.

Then, in May 1987, Stephen King was struck with writer's block.

9

Books, Bangor, and a Rock Band

Stephen King started writing when he was seven and wrote whenever he could. As an adult he wrote every day. Ten years earlier he had commented, "There is a curious loneliness. You have to produce day after day and you have to deal with doubts—that what you're producing is trivial and besides, not even good."[1] Although King still wrote daily, nothing he did between May 1987 and May 1988 was good enough for publication. No short stories were printed that year. No books were written, so fans had no new thrillers to buy in 1988. "Castle Rock" had little news to report, and Stephanie Leonard decided to stop publishing the fan newsletter at the end of 1987. Was Stephen King's reign as King of Horror over?

Absolutely not!

The horror market was still growing. More books were being written, more movies were being made, and more fans were writing letters to Stephen King. Three books about King were published in 1987; four more were printed in 1988. Most analyzed King's stories, the characters, the plots, the settings, and the horror. Some included biographical information and others reprinted interviews. So, although his fans could not read new books *by* Stephen King, they could read seven books *about* him.

In May 1988, one year after it began, King's writer's block lifted. He wrote a short story called "Rainy Season," which was published by *Midnight Graffiti*, a magazine of horror stories.

Other changes soon followed. Three months later it was announced that Kirby McCauley would no longer represent King. No reason was given. Control of King's publishing was put into the hands of his business manager.[2]

The next book, *Nightmares in the Sky*, was a collection of photos of gargoyles from European cathedrals with an essay by King. Of the 250,000 copies printed, 100,000 were returned by bookstores to Viking unsold.[3] Stephen King fans wanted a thriller, not an essay.

In April 1989, the movie *Pet Sematary* opened in Bangor. The audience loved it because King had insisted that it be filmed in Maine. *Pet Sematary* was a box-office success, and King promised to film more of his stories in Maine.

King made other commitments as well. He and his

A portion of Mt. Hope Cemetery in Bangor, Maine, was transformed into a movie set for Pet Sematary.

wife made a donation to the Milton Academy in Massachusetts for its arts and music center, which was named after his mother, Ruth King. The couple pledged half of the $1.5 million needed for an addition to the public library in Old Town, Maine, Tabitha King's hometown.[4] The Kings donated time and money to projects that were important to them and their community.

Once again King was busy. He baked bread and wrote in the morning and handled business in the afternoon. King's secretaries and business office moved out of his house to an old office building near the airport. King set up a small office there to give interviews, talk to the media, and sign letters and books. His secretarial staff answered the fan mail, made travel arrangements, and typed correspondence between King and the outside world.

It took time to respond to five hundred fan letters a week, many from schoolchildren asking questions about King. His secretaries responded with form letters. Many fans requested autographed photographs, but King thought only actors should sign photos. He did sign books, however. King's career had turned around, and Chris Spruce, Tabitha King's brother, decided to publish the "Castle Rock" newsletter for another year.

The wait for a new Stephen King book was finally over in the fall of 1989 when *The Dark Half* arrived in stores. In the book, a writer's pen name comes alive and torments him. King had originally planned to publish this as a Stephen King/Richard Bachman collaboration because of the pen-name plot, but he left Bachman's name off the final draft. He did dedicate the book to the late Richard Bachman. *Publishers Weekly* called *The Dark Half* one of King's best.[5]

In 1989, *Dolan's Cadillac* was published as a limited-edition book. Only one thousand copies were printed, and all were sold before publication.[6] A year later, the complete version of *The Stand* was published. Fans bought the book a second time to read the four hundred pages Doubleday had made King leave out in 1978.

In 1990, the movies based on King's books included *Graveyard Shift* and *Misery*, which won an Academy Award for its star, Kathy Bates. The novel *It* was made into a two-part miniseries for television.

Stephen King was frequently asked to help with fund-raising. Usually, he sent an autographed book to auction off. One time, because he was asked for something he would throw away, he sent a pair of dirty socks.[7] King wrote a short story, "My Pretty Pony," to benefit New York's Whitney Museum of Art. Another time, he appeared at Syracuse University in its "haunted theater" to support its creative writing program. He made fun of the announcements about his appearance. "Stephen King, live on stage." He said, "Raise your hand if you would pay to see me dead."[8] Many hands went up.

Then, in 1991, the Kings had a personal experience with horror. Early one morning, an ex-convict from Texas broke into their Bangor home. He threatened Tabitha King with what appeared to be a bomb. Still in her nightgown, she ran out the back door and called the police from a neighbor's phone. The police arrested him. The bomb turned out to be fake, made of cardboard and some electronic parts from a calculator. When questioned, the man said he wanted King to buy him contact lenses, beer, and cigarettes and to help him write a book. He pleaded not guilty by reason of insanity, though the case never went to trial.[9]

The same month, a woman from New Jersey filed a lawsuit against Stephen King. She claimed that he had broken into her home and a storage room with the cooperation of the local police and that he had flown over her home in an airplane and eavesdropped with a listening device. She also claimed King had burglarized her more than 150 times in 1990 and had published her manuscripts as his own.[10] The lawsuit was dismissed.

The year 1991 saw the publication of *Four Past Midnight*, *The Dark Tower III: The Waste Lands*, and *Needful Things*. King was regularly publishing two or more novels a year. *Needful Things* was the final book set in Castle Rock. Throughout the tale, characters from other Castle Rock stories come back, including some that had been killed off. Even Cujo is back.

In 1992 the Greater Bangor Chamber of Commerce honored Stephen and Tabitha King with the Norbert X. Dowd Award for community service. During an interview with the *Bangor Daily News*, King said, "Whatever we've done for Bangor was the result of what Bangor had done for us."[11]

Stephen King has always liked music. He had bought, sold, and rebought WZON, the Bangor radio station, so he could hear the music he liked any time of day. He plays the guitar, and he decided to join a band in 1992. Made up mostly of writers, the band was called "The Rock Bottom Remainders." (Remainders are unsold books that are sent back to the publishers.) The first performance of the group was at a gathering of the American Booksellers Association in Anaheim, California. The original group included humorist Dave Barry, lead guitar and vocals; writer Michael Dorris, percussion; cartoonist Matt Groening, backup vocals; writer Barbara Kingsolver, keyboards and vocals; and writer Amy Tan, chorus. Stephen King played the rhythm guitar and added vocals. With only three days to rehearse before their first performance, they learned songs such as "Louie Louie," "Bye, Bye Love," and "Take Out Some Insurance." They were a hit in Anaheim, but as for their future, Dave Barry said, "The band plays music as well as [the band] Metallica writes novels."[12]

Next came two books that featured strong female characters, *Gerald's Game* (1992) and *Dolores Claiborne* (1993). *Nightmares and Dreamscapes*, also published in 1993, was a collection of short stories that included "Heads Down," the account of his son's Little League team winning the state championship.

Stephen King always loved baseball, and the project for which he may best be remembered in his new hometown is the Bangor baseball stadium. Built on the parkland behind his home, Mansfield Stadium, nicknamed the Field of Screams, started with a $1 million donation from King. Community members donated the rest, and the field was completed in 1993 for the children of Bangor. When the local minor-league baseball team asked to rent the facility, they were told no because it was only for children.

The Rock Bottom Remainders regrouped in 1993 to raise money for adult literacy programs that teach people to read. Their "3 Chords and an Attitude Tour" performed in eight cities. Tabitha King went along as tour photographer to record this experience for future generations. Fans loved seeing a musical side of their favorite authors.

The movie *Sleepwalkers* (1994), like most of King's stories, was inspired by a real-life experience: His son wanted to date a girl working at a popcorn stand. She was an all-American girl after whom King patterned

Batter up! On the pitcher's mound at the new Mansfield Stadium is Stephen King, who donated $1 million to help build the stadium for the children of Bangor.

one of the characters. Also in 1994, *The Stand* and two of King's short stories, "Sometimes They Come Back" and "Golden Years," were shown on television.

That same year, when *Insomnia*—a story about an old man who wakes up an hour earlier each day—hit the shelves, Stephen King hit the road. In appreciation of the support the independent bookstores gave him, King hopped on his Harley-Davidson motorcycle in Bangor. For three weeks and 4,690 miles, he stopped at independent bookstores across the United States, autographing books and participating in question-and-answer sessions. People were nice to him wherever he went. During a snowstorm in Wyoming, strangers gave him a gadget to warm his gloves and boots. One rainy night, the desk clerk of a motel let King park his Harley in her garage.[13]

King spent part of his *Insomnia* tour doing research for a future novel. In 1991 while driving his daughter's car to the West Coast, he had passed through Ruth, Nevada. The town seemed deserted, but it was obvious that people lived there. King asked himself, what if all the people were dead? On his 1994 motorcycle tour, he stopped in Ruth again to learn more about the town.

A crowd greeted Stephen King in Santa Cruz, California, his last stop. During the question-and-answer session, whenever King mentioned a title of one of his books, the audience erupted in applause.[14] Then he put the Harley in a van for shipping and he flew back to Bangor.

Rose Madder was published in 1995. In this story,

Rosie Daniels, an abused wife, escapes into the magical world of a painting and becomes Rose Madder.

Sometimes, filmmakers buy the rights to use titles from old films and make a sequel, hoping people will pay to see it because of its connection to the original movie. Few sequels of King's movies were written by him or even approved by him. He did work on *Creepshow 2*, but he had nothing to do with *Lawnmower Man 2*, *Pet Sematary 2*, or any of the *Children of the Corn* sequels.

The Kings continued to support their community and programs they felt were important. When Stephen King donated money to the Durham Elementary School, the accompanying note read, "Get 'em some great stories." When the Kings heard that the athletic budget was cut at University of Maine, Orono, they donated money to support the men's and women's varsity swimming and diving programs. Eastern Medical Center benefited from a generous donation to build a new pediatrics wing, and Stephen King acted as the honorary chairman. He wrote letters telling people about the addition and asking for their support.

Two books resulted from King's trips through Nevada: *Desperation*, by Stephen King, and *The Regulators*, by King but published under the pen name Richard Bachman. The books are like fraternal twins, published on the same day—September 24, 1996. Both books feature a broken-down writer whose output has decreased. In *Desperation*, the main character rides his motorcycle, a Harley-Davidson, across the country. The books have the same setting,

Stephen King poses alongside the poster for Creepshow 2, *the movie sequel based on his stories.*

share a few passages word for word, and feature some of the same characters but from different points of view. On both covers is art by the same artist. When the books are held side by side, their covers merge to make a complete picture.[15] Dutton, the publisher of *The Regulators*, advertised that Richard Bachman had died in 1985, but his widow had found the manuscript in her attic.

Meanwhile, Tabitha King became the honorary chairman of the Bangor Library renovation project. The impressive stone building in downtown Bangor, was in need of extensive work. The Kings gave a generous donation to start the repairs. The library relocated to an old manufacturing building outside town while the improvements were made that would bring state-of-the-art media services to the Bangor community.

The first volume of *The Green Mile*, which was written and published in six installments, was released in March 1996. King wanted to write a serial novel like those Charles Dickens had written more than a century before. Readers had no way of knowing that master storyteller Stephen King had written most of the second chapter during a rain delay at a baseball game.[16]

After Viking published *Rose Madder* and *Desperation*, King had no further commitments for any books. He decided it was time to look for a new publisher, one who might give him some benefits that Viking could not. King's search was followed closely by the literary world. Rumors started: He was being unreasonably demanding; he was jealous of a rival

Stephen and Tabitha King accept the Norbert X. Dowd Award for community service. "Whatever we've done for Bangor was the result of what Bangor had done for us," said Stephen King.

who might be earning more than he was; he was not able to sell books as he once did.[17]

The first week in November 1997, King signed with Simon & Schuster, which offered him a fresh and imaginative publishing plan and a campaign to increase his readership. The Scribner division would publish King's hardback books, Pocket Books would produce the paperbacks, and Simon & Schuster Audio would record the books on tape. Having all three forms of publication under one publisher might make contracts and publishing schedules easier to deal with.[18]

Three books were immediately planned with his new publisher. *Bag of Bones*, the story of a Maine novelist who has writer's block as a result of the death of his wife, was released in 1998. *Hearts in Atlantis*, a collection of related short stories, was published the following year. The third book in the contract would be a nonfiction book about writing.

Simon & Schuster wanted to get Stephen King back in contact with the readers who love him. The publisher arranged for two tours following the release of *Bag of Bones*. King went first to England, then around the United States, signing books and making a personal connection with fans. At the same time, King appeared on several television shows to promote his new book. Simon & Schuster also kept the public informed of King's writing and appearances through its Web page on the Internet. In February 1999, the Web site announced a contest. Twenty-five fans would win a copy of the screenplay of "Storm of the Century," a television miniseries that aired that month on ABC. Those who entered but did not win could buy copies of the script in paperback at bookstores.

To promote "Storm of the Century," King appeared on three television shows and a radio program on a single day. His humor and spontaneous horror stories thrilled the live audiences as well as the viewing and listening audiences. During one show he danced. On another he explained his fears of flying and the number thirteen. Stephen King was fifty-one and still talking about having the heart of a small boy.

King continued to participate in fund-raising activities that were important to him. In 1998 he had appeared for the second time on *Jeopardy*, winning thousands of dollars for charity. He also appeared with the Rock Bottom Remainders at several American Booksellers Association conventions. The members of the band varied, depending on which musical writers attended the gatherings.

King surprised his publisher and his fans by writing *The Girl Who Loved Tom Gordon*. The unexpected story was released in April 1999 and was about a nine-year-old girl lost in the Maine woods. What keeps her alive through the fear and the terror is her love of the Boston Red Sox relief pitcher Tom Gordon, whose games she listens to on her radio.

A dog was responsible for the real-life horror Stephen King experienced in June 1999. He was walking along a rural Maine highway near Sebago Lake when a motorist, distracted by his dog, lost control of his van. The van went off the road, striking King and throwing him fourteen feet. King had major injuries that included a collapsed lung, broken ribs, and multiple fractures of his right leg and hip. He suffered through several surgeries and would require a lengthy rehabilitation. King's office posted regular updates on his condition in newspapers and on his Web site. They reported that his serious injuries were from the shoulders down, his mental state remained excellent, and his ability to write would not be affected.

By the end of the twentieth century, Stephen King had sold more books than any other American author. Meanwhile, books *about* Stephen King continued to be published. Some educators realized that King's work could improve the reading skills of teenagers, so they developed curriculum guides to go along with a few of his novels.

Not all of King's writing is horror fiction. He won the prestigious O. Henry Award, which is given to honor literary short fiction, for "The Man in the Black Suit." Originally published in *The New Yorker*, this story has just a hint of the supernatural. Two short stories, "Do the Dead Sing?" and "Uncle Otto's Truck," have appeared in *Yankee*, a family magazine. He once started a western but gave up when he discovered the most interesting part was when the town drunk fell into the pig sty and was being eaten by the pigs. He admitted that one morning he might wake up and want to write about something ordinary.[19] The question is, would a publisher print it?

King is often asked where he gets his ideas. He has several creative answers: "I get mine in Utica." "There's a great little bookstore on Forty-second Street in New York called Used Ideas. I go there when I run dry." "I get them at 239 Center Street in Bangor, just around the corner from the Frati Brothers Pawnshop."[20]

Readers know where Stephen King gets his ideas. They come from his experiences, from asking "What if?" and from his imagination.[21] Who could imagine that a bathtub in Room 217, a Plymouth Fury he once owned, and a close encounter with a Saint Bernard dog would develop into best-sellers. Ideas are everywhere, and Stephen King is not afraid to let them find him.

Stephen King's Legacy

Horror scenes have been part of literature for centuries. In the *Odyssey*, the ancient-Greek poet Homer tells of Odysseus poking out the eye of Cyclops with a huge, burning club. Homer describes in gory detail how the eye bubbled and hissed. Two thousand years later, *Beowulf*, an epic poem written in Old English, followed the adventures of a mighty warrior. In his attempt to help the Danish king, Beowulf is stranded in a room with many people. Each night a strange mist floats in and kills some of them. In the early 1600s, Shakespeare wrote *Hamlet*, a dramatic horror story that included blood, fear, death, and a ghost. These are now considered classics, studied by students and analyzed by scholars.

Three horror books from the 1800s, Mary Shelley's *Frankenstein,* Bram Stoker's *Dracula,* and Robert Louis Stevenson's *The Strange Case of Dr. Jekyll and Mr. Hyde,* have been read, studied, taught, and made into movies and plays. They, too, are now considered classics.

Classics are stories that survive, that still bring pleasure and offer entertainment years after they are written. Will any of Stephen King's novels become classics? No one knows for sure, but consider this: *Carrie* was still being sold more than twenty-five years after its first printing. Other King stories have been just as popular. Many readers say that a Stephen King novel was the first book they ever read from cover to cover and really enjoyed.

When asked whether he thought children should read horror stories, King answered, "I don't know. I did, and it warped me really good."[1] He was joking, of course. King's personal life does not seem warped. He has been married to Tabitha since 1971, has raised three children, has contributed time and money to improve his community, and has written books that entertain millions of readers each year. King has said, "I was raised to please people. That was one of the things my mother taught me to do."[2]

Believe it or not, Stephen King had trouble pleasing photographers because he was rather ordinary-looking. They would ask him to do something spooky and then take pictures that made him look the way they wanted. "I'm doing the best I can with what I've got," King once explained. [3]

The "Castle Rock" newsletter ceased publication in

Stephen King, a 1970 graduate, was invited back to the University of Maine, Orono, to speak at the graduation ceremony in 1987.

1989, so fans have had to find other ways to learn about Stephen King's life and works. Some of his biggest fans have created Stephen King Web pages. With just a click, anyone with an Internet connection can visit these pages and download pictures and other information about him. These fan pages are not authorized by King, and the information may not be accurate. To counteract the many errors, Stephen King and his staff created an official Web site <www.stephenking.com> in December 1998.

Stephen King appreciates his fans and is happy to autograph their books, but it is a complicated, time-consuming process. To get a book autographed, readers must send a written request to King's business office. His secretary will reply by mail, telling when to send the book to Bangor. King has many requests for autographs, so the waiting period is often more than a year. Books sent without permission are returned. King's secretary keeps track of those who request autographs, because King has a strict policy. He will give only one autograph per person.

Stephen King's tales will be remembered in other ways. A majestic walnut tree grew on the ranch in Petaluma, California, where the movie *Cujo* was filmed. The tree died of old age in the mid-1990s. When the tree was cut down, the wood was used by Taylor Guitars to make the backs and sides of 250 limited-edition guitars. King gave the company permission to use the name Cujo, and he autographed stickers that were placed inside each guitar. The fingerboard of the guitar was inlaid with the figure of Cujo near the neck with walnut tree branches weaving

Rocking writers: Stephen King performs with the Rock Bottom Remainders. "The band plays music as well as Metallica writes novels," says humorist Dave Barry, another of the literary musicians.

through the frets past a barn and into a full moon. King has Cujo guitar number one.

Stephen King has said that his life goals include being a good husband, being a good father, and staying alive.[4] He may not be remembered for achieving these particular goals, but he has already looked ahead to the time he dies. His epitaph will say, "It is the tale, not he who tells it."[5] Nothing else. No name or dates. Imagine the thoughts of a twelve-year-old child sitting on the wall of a cemetery looking at this stone. King looked at tombstones and wondered why so many had died so young. This child may wonder if it is the writer or his story that is buried. But both the writer and his stories are bound to live long after the tombstone is in place—either on bookshelves or in people's minds.

When asked what he read when he wanted to be frightened, King replied, "The *New York Times*."[6] What is more horrifying than war, starvation, and cancer? Not horror books, because readers can put them back on the shelf whenever they choose. Not horror movies, because viewers know a zipper is hidden in the monster suit. So why are horror tales so popular if people know they are phony? As King explains it, "We make up horrors to help us cope with the real ones."[7] If fighting vampires, ghosts in bathtubs, and mad dogs on the printed page or on a movie screen helps people handle the problems and challenges in their lives, then it is no wonder that horror stories, especially Stephen King tales, are so popular.

Chronology

(See page 112 for a list of Stephen King books.)

1947— Stephen Edwin King is born September 21 in Portland, Maine.

1949— Father, Donald King, deserts the family.

1953— King family moves to Stratford, Connecticut.

1954— Stephen writes his first science fiction story, about a dinosaur destroying the world.

1958— The King family moves to Durham, Maine, so Stephen's mother can take care of her parents.

1959— Stephen, his brother, and his cousin publish a neighborhood newspaper called "Dave's Rag"; Stephen starts writing daily and submits stories to various magazines.

1963— Stephen writes high school sports stories for the *Lisbon Enterprise*.

1965— Stephen receives his first acceptance, for the story "I Was a Teenage Grave Robber."

1966— King writes his first novel, *Getting It On*, the summer before he enrolls at the University of Maine, Orono.

1970— King graduates from the University of Maine and goes to work first at a gas station and then at a laundry; several short stories are accepted for publication.

1971— King marries Tabitha Spruce and they move to Herman, Maine, where he gets a teaching job.

1973— *Carrie* is accepted by Doubleday; King's mother dies.

1974— *Carrie* is published; the Kings move to Boulder, Colorado, for a year; a visit to the Stanley Hotel inspires *The Shining.*

1975— *'Salem's Lot* is published. The Kings move to Long Lake in Bridgton, Maine.

1976— *Carrie* is made into a movie; King meets Kirby McCauley, who becomes his literary agent; King breaks his association with Doubleday Publishers.

1977— *The Shining* becomes a best-seller; *Rage* is published under King's pen name, Richard Bachman; the Kings live in England for three months, then buy a house in Center Lovell, Maine.

1978— King is a visiting professor, teaching creative writing at the University of Maine, Orono.

1980— The Kings buy a 129-year-old house in Bangor, Maine.

1982— Receives the Hugo Award for Best Nonfiction of the Year for *Danse Macabre* and the World Fantasy Award for "Do the Dead Sing?"; named best fiction writer of the year by *US* magazine.

1983— Buys a Bangor radio station and renames it WZON.

1985— The first issue of "Castle Rock," the Stephen King newsletter, is printed; Richard Bachman is revealed to be Stephen King; five of his books appear on national best-seller lists at the same time, a record for any author so far.

1987— King suffers writer's block.

1988— King's writer's block lifts in May; he receives the Bram Stoker Award for *Misery*.

1992— Stephen and Tabitha King receive the Norbert X. Dowd Award for community service; King is a founding member of the band called the Rock Bottom Remainders.

1993— The Rock Bottom Remainders go on tour to raise money for adult literacy.

1994— King tours the country on his motorcycle to promote the newly published book *Insomnia*; "The Man in the Black Suit" wins an O. Henry Award and a World Fantasy award; King wins the Bram Stoker Award for "Lunch at the Gotham Café."

1997— King signs with Simon & Schuster.

1999— King makes numerous public appearances to promote "Storm of the Century"; is seriously injured in June when he is hit by a van; begins a long physical recovery and resumes writing a little each day.

Books by Stephen King

Carrie, 1974
'Salem's Lot, 1975
Rage, 1977 (Bachman)
The Shining, 1977
Night Shift, 1978
    Short stories, including
    "The Lawnmower Man"
    "Children of the Corn"
The Stand, 1978
The Long Walk, 1979 (Bachman)
The Dead Zone, 1979
Firestarter, 1980
Roadwork, 1981 (Bachman)
Cujo, 1981
Danse Macabre, 1981
Creepshow, 1982
The Running Man, 1982 (Bachman)
The Dark Tower: The Gunslinger, 1982
Different Seasons, 1982
    Four short novels:
    "Rita Hayworth and Shawshank Redemption"
    "Apt Pupil"
    "The Body"
    "The Breathing Method"
Christine, 1983

Cycle of the Werewolf, 1983
Pet Sematary, 1983
The Talisman, 1984 (with Peter Straub)
Thinner, 1984 (Bachman)
Skeleton Crew, 1985
    Short stories, including
    "The Mist"
    "Here There Be Tygers"
It, 1986
The Dark Tower II: The Drawing of Three, 1987
The Eyes of the Dragon, 1987
Misery, 1987
The Tommyknockers, 1987
The Dark Half, 1989
The Stand; The Complete & Uncut Edition, 1990
Four Past Midnight, 1990
    Four short novels:
    "The Langoliers"
    "Secret Window, Secret Garden"
    "The Library Policeman"
    "The Sun Dog"
The Dark Tower III: The Wastelands, 1991
Needful Things, 1991
Gerald's Game, 1992
Dolores Claiborne, 1993
Nightmares & Dreamscapes, 1993
    Short stories, including
    "Dolan's Cadillac"
    "My Pretty Pony"
Insomnia, 1994
Rose Madder, 1995
Desperation, 1996
The Regulators, 1996 (Bachman)

The Green Mile, 1996
>   Six parts:
>   "The Two Dead Girls"
>   "The Mouse on the Mile"
>   "Coffey's Hands"
>   "The Bad Death of Eduard Delacroix"
>   "Night Journey"
>   "Coffey on the Mile"

The Dark Tower IV: Wizard and Glass, 1997

Bag of Bones, 1998

Storm of the Century, 1999
>   Original tale written for television

The Girl Who Loved Tom Gordon, 1999

Hearts in Atlantis, 1999
>   Collection of short stories about the sixties

Chapter Notes

Chapter 1. Horror at the Stanley Hotel

1. George Beahm, *The Stephen King Story* (Kansas City, Mo.: Andrews & McMeel, 1991), p. 69.

2. Ibid.

3. Mel Allen, "The Man Who Writes Nightmares," *Yankee*, March 1979, p. 124.

4. Ibid.

5. Beahm, p. 69.

6. Allen, p. 124.

7. Beahm, p. 69.

8. Ibid., p. 68.

9. Ibid., p. 69.

10. Mark Schwed, "The Shining—It Lives Again," *TV Guide*, April 26–May 2, 1997, p. 21.

11. Ibid.

Chapter 2. Tastes of Terror

1. George Beahm, *The Stephen King Story* (Kansas City, Mo.: Andrews & McMeel, 1991), p. 15.

2. Mel Allen, "The Man Who Writes Nightmares," *Yankee*, March 1979, p. 87.

3. Eric Norden, "Stephen King," *Playboy*, June 1983, p. 82.

4. Stephen J. Spignesi, "Interview with David King," in Stephen J. Spignesi, ed., *The Complete Stephen King Encyclopedia*, (Chicago: Contemporary Books, Inc., 1991), p. 32.

5. Ibid.

6. Christopher Evans, "He Brings Life to Dead Issues," *Minneapolis Star*, September 8, 1979, reprinted in Tim Underwood and Chuck Miller, eds., *Bare Bones* (New York: McGraw-Hill Book Co., 1988), p. 90.

7. Stephen King, *Danse Macabre* (New York: Berkley Books, 1981), p. 83.

8. Spignesi, p. 32.

9. King, p. 118.

10. Beahm, p. 17.

11. Ibid.

12. King, pp. 97–99.

13. Beahm, p. 18.

14. Ibid., p. 17.

15. Bob Spitz, "Penthouse Interview: Stephen King," *Penthouse*, April 1982, reprinted in Underwood and Miller, eds., *Bare Bones*, pp. 186–187.

16. Allen, p. 87.

17. Tim Underwood and Chuck Miller, *Kingdom of Fear: The World of Stephen King* (Columbia, Pa.: Underwood and Miller, 1986), p. 187.

18. Allen, p. 87.

19. George Beahm, ed., *The Stephen King Companion* (Kansas City, Mo.: Andrews & McMeel, 1989), p. 103.

20. Beahm, *The Stephen King Story*, p. 16.

21. Matt Schaffer, "Interview with Stephen King," broadcast by WBCN-FM Radio's *Boston Sunday Review*, October 31, 1983, reprinted in Underwood and Miller, eds., *Bare Bones*, p. 115.

22. Michael Kilgore, "Interview with Stephen King," *The Tampa Tribune*, August 31, 1980, reprinted in Underwood and Miller, eds., *Bare Bones*, p. 103.

Chapter 3. Moving Around

1. Stephen King, *Danse Macabre* (New York: Berkley Books, 1981), p. 108.

2. Ibid.

3. Letter to the author from Stephen King, March 22, 1999.

4. George Beahm, *The Stephen King Story* (Kansas City, Mo.: Andrews & McMeel, 1991), p. 19.

5. King, p. 90.

6. Ibid., p. 109.

7. Ibid., p. 110.

8. Mel Allen, "The Man Who Writes Nightmares," *Yankee*, March 1979, p. 84.

9. *Brunswick Record*, April 23, 1959, reprinted in Stephen J. Spignesi, ed., *The Complete Stephen King Encyclopedia* (Chicago: Contemporary Books, Inc., 1991), p. 41.

10. "Interview with David King," in Spignesi, p. 32.

11. "Dave's Rag," reprinted in Spignesi, p. 46.

12. Ibid., p. 44.

13. "Interview with Chris Chesley," in Spignesi, p. 56.

14. Ibid., p. 59.

15. Spignesi, p. 467.

16. Letter to the author from Stephen King, March 22, 1999.

17. "Interview with Chris Chesley," in Spignesi, p. 52.

18. "Interview with David King," in Spignesi, p. 32.

19. Christopher Chesley, "Death Scenes," in Spignesi, pp. 583–584.

20. Ibid.

21. King, pp. 94–95.

22. Ibid., p. 95.

23. Mel Allen, "Witches and Aspirin," *Writer's Digest*, June 1977, p. 27.

Chapter 4. Education and Rejection

1. Christopher Chesley, "Death Scenes," in Stephen J. Spignesi, ed., *The Complete Stephen King Encyclopedia* (Chicago: Contemporary Books, Inc., 1991), p. 582.

2. "Interview with Chris Chesley," in Spignesi, p. 58.

3. Keith Bellows, "The King of Terror," *Sourcebook*, 1982, by 13-30 Corporation, reprinted in Tim Underwood and Chuck Miller, eds., *Bare Bones* (New York: McGraw-Hill Book Co., 1988), pp. 89–90.

4. Letter to the author from Stephen King, March 22, 1999.

5. Joyce Lynch Dewes Moore, "An Interview with Stephen King," *Mystery*, March 1981, reprinted in Underwood and Miller, *Bare Bones*, p. 72.

6. Stanley Wiater and Roger Anker, 1984 World Fantasy Convention, Ottawa, Canada, interview reprinted in Underwood and Miller, *Bare Bones*, p. 177.

7. George Beahm, *The Stephen King Story* (Kansas City, Mo.: Andrews & McMeel, 1991), p. 30.

8. Stephen King, "My First Car," *Gentlemen's Quarterly*, July 1984.

9. Beahm, p. 32.

10. Ibid., p. 33.

11. Ibid., p. 35.

12. Stephen King, "Garbage Truck," *The Maine Campus*, April 30, 1970, p. 5.

13. Beahm, p. 50.

14. Ibid., p. 40.

15. Mel Allen, "The Man Who Writes Nightmares," *Yankee*, March 1979, p. 87.

16. Beahm, p. 47.

17. "Interview with Chris Chesley," in Spignesi, p. 52.

18. Stephen King, "On Becoming a Brand Name," *Adelina*, February 1980, reprinted in Tim Underwood and Chuck Miller, eds., *Fear Itself* (San Francisco: Underwood and Miller, 1982), p. 16.

19. Allen, p. 87.

20. Beahm, p. 44.

21. Personal interview with Marsha DeFilippo, Stephen King's secretary, October 29, 1997.

Chapter 5. A Breakthrough Sale

1. Eric Norden, "Stephen King," *Playboy*, June 1983, p. 72.

2. Personal interview with Thomas Bailey, president, New Franklin Textile Services, October 30, 1997.

3. Stephen J. Spignesi, "Interview with Chris Chesley," Stephen J. Spignesi, ed., *The Complete Stephen King Encyclopedia* (Chicago: Contemporary Books, Inc., 1991), p. 53.

4. Stephen King, *The Bachman Books: Four Early Novels by Stephen King* (New York.: NAL Books, 1985), p. v.

5. Burton Hatlen, "Stephen King and the American Dream: Alienation, Competition, and Community in *Rage* and *The Long Walk*," in Don Herron, ed., *Reign of Fear* (Novato, Calif.: Underwood and Miller, 1992), p. 22.

6. Mel Allen, "The Man Who Writes Nightmares," *Yankee*, March 1979, p. 84.

7. Tim Underwood and Chuck Miller, eds., *Fear Itself* (San Francisco: Underwood and Miller, 1982), p. 19.

8. Joyce Lynch Dewes Moore, "An Interview with Stephen King," *Mystery*, March 1981, reprinted in Tim Underwood and Chuck Miller, eds., *Bare Bones* (New York: McGraw-Hill Book Co., 1988), p. 73.

9. Underwood and Miller, *Fear Itself*, p. 18.

10. Tim Underwood and Chuck Miller, *Kingdom of Fear: The World of Stephen King* (Columbia, Pa.: Underwood and Miller, 1986), p. 31.

11. Charles L. Grant, "Interview with Stephen King," *Monsterland Magazine*, May and June 1985, reprinted in Underwood and Miller, *Bare Bones*, p. 86.

12. Moore, p. 72.

13. Underwood and Miller, *Fear Itself*, p. 25.

14. Underwood and Miller, *Kingdom of Fear*, p. 33.

15. Underwood and Miller, *Fear Itself*, p. 25.

16. Underwood and Miller, *Kingdom of Fear*, p. 29.

17. Underwood and Miller, *Fear Itself*, p. 26.

18. Beahm, p. 62.

19. Moore, p. 75.

20. Mel Allen, "Witches and Aspirin," *Writer's Digest*, June 1977, p. 27.

21. Underwood and Miller, *Fear Itself*, p. 28.

22. *60 Minutes*, CBS-TV, February 16, 1997, transcript, p. 5.

23. Beahm, p. 64.

Chapter 6. A Growing Reputation

1. George Beahm, *The Stephen King Story* (Kansas City, Mo.: Andrews & McMeel, 1991), p. 64.

2. Ibid., p. 65.

3. Ibid., p. 66.

4. Ibid., p. 67.

5. Tim Underwood and Chuck Miller, eds., *Fear Itself* (San Francisco: Underwood and Miller, 1982), p. 37.

6. Joyce Lynch Dewes Moore, "An Interview with Stephen King," *Mystery*, March 1981, reprinted in Tim Underwood and Chuck Miller, eds., *Bare Bones* (New York: McGraw-Hill Book Co., 1988), p. 74.

7. Ibid., p. 75.

8. Beahm, p. 68.

9. Moore, p. 74.

10. Beahm, pp. 70–71.

11. Mel Allen, "Witches and Aspirin," *Writer's Digest,* June 1977, p. 27.

12. Beahm, p. 77.

13. Ibid.

14. Ibid., p. 79.

Chapter 7. A Maine Writer

1. Tim Underwood and Chuck Miller, *Kingdom of Fear: The World of Stephen King* (Columbia, Pa.: Underwood and Miller, 1986), p. 110.

2. George Beahm, *The Stephen King Story* (Kansas City, Mo.: Andrews & McMeel, 1991), p. 56.

3. Ibid., p. 80.

4. Ibid.

5. Ibid., p. 81.

6. Ibid.

7. Stanley Wiater and Roger Anker, "Three Interviews with Stephen King and Peter Straub," Interview 3, *Valley Advocate*, October 31, 1984, reprinted in Tim Underwood and Chuck Miller, eds., *Bare Bones* (New York: McGraw-Hill Book Co., 1988), p. 171.

8. Beahm, p. 83.

9. Ibid., p. 86.

10. Ibid.

11. Ibid.

12. Joyce Lynch Dewes Moore, "An Interview with Stephen King," *Mystery*, March 1981, reprinted in Tim Underwood and Chuck Miller, eds., *Bare Bones* (New York: McGraw-Hill Book Co., 1988), pp. 68–69.

Chapter 8. Writing in a Haunted House

1. George Beahm, ed., *The Stephen King Companion* (Kansas City, Mo.: Andrews & McMeel, 1989), p. 79.

2. George Beahm, *The Stephen King Story* (Kansas City, Mo.: Andrews & McMeel, 1991), p. 93.

3. Charles L. Grant, "Interview with Stephen King," *Monsterland Magazine*, May and June 1985, reprinted in Tim Underwood and Chuck Miller, eds., *Bare Bones* (New York: McGraw-Hill Book Co., 1988), p. 80.

4. Edwin Pouncy, "Would You Buy a Haunted Car from This Man?" *Sounds*, May 21, 1983, reprinted in Underwood and Miller, *Bare Bones*, p. 58.

5. Grant, p. 81.

6. Keith Bellows, "The King of Terror," *Sourcebook*, 1982 by 13–30 Corporation, reprinted in Underwood and Miller, *Bare Bones*, p. 89.

7. Beahm, *The Stephen King Companion*, p. 112.

8. Stephen J. Spignesi, *The Complete Stephen King Encyclopedia* (Chicago: Contemporary Books, 1991), p. 551.

9. Beahm, *The Stephen King Story*, p. 113.

10. Joel Denver, "Stephen King Takes a Stand for Records," *Radio and Records*, February 24, 1984, reprinted in Underwood and Miller, *Bare Bones*, p. 194.

11. Ibid., p. 196.

12. Beahm, *The Stephen King Story*, p. 127.

13. Don Herron, ed., *Reign of Fear* (Novato, Calif.: Underwood and Miller, 1992), pp. xi–xii.

14. Spignesi, p. 22.

15. Eric Norden, "Stephen King," *Playboy*, June 1983, p. 66.

16. Beahm, *The Stephen King Story*, p. 121.

17. Ibid., p. 123.

Chapter 9. Books, Bangor, and a Rock Band

1. Mel Allen, "Witches and Aspirin," *Writer's Digest*, June 1977, p. 27.

2. George Beahm, *The Stephen King Story* (Kansas City, Mo.: Andrews & McMeel, 1991), p. 143.

3. Ibid., p. 142.

4. Ibid., p. 146.

5. Ibid., pp. 147–148.

6. Ibid., pp. 144–145.

7. Stephen J. Spignesi, "Interview with Stephanie Leonard," in Stephen J. Spignesi, ed., *The Complete Stephen King Encyclopedia* (Chicago: Contemporary Books, Inc., 1991), p. 100.

8. Anthony Timpone, ed., *Fangoria: Masters of the Dark* (New York: Harper Prism, 1997), p. 69.

9. Ibid., pp. 75–76.

10. Ibid., p. 76.

11. Beahm, *The Stephen King Story*, p. 191.

12. "Rock Bottom Remainders," *"Don't Quit Your Day Job" Records*, April 19, 1999, <http://www.dqydj.com/rbr.htm> (November 25, 1996).

13. Michael Berry, "Stephen King's Misery," *San Diego Union-Tribune*, November 3, 1994, p. E-1.

14. Ibid.

15. Judy Quinn, "King of the Season," *Publishers Weekly*, August 5, 1996, pp. 293–294.

16. Bruce Handy, "Monster Writer," *Time*, September 2, 1996, p. 61.

17. Martin Arnold, "Getting Spooked by King's Tactic," *The New York Times*, November 5, 1997, p. E3.

18. "Stephen King Partners with Simon and Schuster Companies," Simon & Schuster Company Press Release, <http://biz.yahoo.com/prnews/97/11/06/via_y0026_1.html> (November 6, 1997).

19. Stephen Jones, "The Night Shifter," *Fantasy Media*, March 1979, reprinted in Tim Underwood and Chuck Miller, eds., *Bare Bones* (New York: McGraw-Hill Book Co., 1988), p. 119.

20. George Beahm, ed., *The Stephen King Companion* (Kansas City, Mo.: Andrews & McMeel, 1989), p. 161.

21. Ibid., p. 155.

Chapter 10. Stephen King's Legacy

1. Charles L. Grant, "Interview with Stephen King," *Monsterland Magazine*, May and June 1985, reprinted in Tim Underwood and Chuck Miller, eds., *Bare Bones* (New York: McGraw Hill Book Co., 1988), p. 88.

2. Jo Fletcher, "Stephen King: The Limits of Fear," *Knave*, vol. 19, no. 5, 1987, reprinted in Don Herron, ed., *Reign of Fear* (Novato, Calif.: Underwood and Miller, 1992), p. x.

3. *60 Minutes*, CBS-TV, February 16, 1997, transcript, p. 6.

4. Stanley Wiater and Roger Anker, 1984 World Fantasy Convention, Ottawa, Canada, interview reprinted in Underwood and Miller, *Bare Bones*, p. 177.

5. Eric Norden, "Stephen King," *Playboy*, June 1983, p. 239.

6. George Beahm, *The Stephen King Story* (Kansas City, Mo.: Andrews & McMeel, 1991), p. 166.

7. Stephen King, *Danse Macabre* (New York: Berkley Books, 1981), p. 13.

Further Reading

Beahm, George. *Stephen King: America's Best-Loved Boogeyman.* Kansas City, Mo.: Andrews & McMeel Publishing, 1998.

———. *Stephen King: A to Z.* Kansas City, Mo.: Andrews & McMeel, 1998.

———. *Stephen King Country.* Philadelphia: Running Press, 1999.

Keyishian, Amy, and Marjorie Keyishian. *Stephen King.* New York: Chelsea House, 1996.

King, Stephen. *Danse Macabre.* New York: Berkeley Books, 1981.

Russell, Sharon A. *Stephen King: A Critical Companion.* Westport, Conn.: Greenwood Press, 1996.

Saidman, Anne. *Stephen King: Master of Horror.* Minneapolis: Lerner Publications, 1992.

Spignesi, Stephen J., ed. *The Complete Stephen King Encyclopedia.* Chicago: Contemporary Books, Inc., 1991.

——— *The Lost Work of Stephen King.* Secaucus, N.J.: Carol Publishing Group, 1998.

Underwood, Tim, and Chuck Miller, eds. *Bare Bones.* New York: McGraw-Hill Book Co., 1988.

Wukovits, John F. *Stephen King.* San Diego, Calif.: Lucent Books, 1999.

Internet Addresses

Authorized Stephen King Web Page
<http://www.stephenking.com>

Stephen King Links

<http://www.southsideweb.com/stephenking/sklinks.htm>

The Stephen King Library

<http://www.stephenkinglibrary.com/>

Index